# The Ancient Fathers

## ON THE OFFICE AND WORK OF THE PRIESTHOOD IN THE CHURCH OF CHRIST.

# The Ancient Fathers

## ON THE OFFICE AND WORK OF THE PRIESTHOOD
## IN THE CHURCH OF CHRIST.

BEING AN ENGLISH TRANSLATION OF A PRINCIPAL PORTION OF
A WORK PUBLISHED UNDER THE TITLE OF "DU SACERDOCE,"
BY "A DIRECTOR OF THE SEMINARY," IN LATIN AND FRENCH.

*(Paris, Vivès, 1857.)*

*Dedicated by his Lordship's kind permission to*

EDWARD, LORD BISHOP OF LINCOLN,

AND FORMERLY PROFESSOR OF PASTORAL THEOLOGY
IN THE UNIVERSITY OF OXFORD.

WIPF & STOCK · Eugene, Oregon

Wipf and Stock Publishers
199 W 8th Ave, Suite 3
Eugene, OR 97401

The Ancient Fathers on the Office and Work of the
Priesthood in the Church of Christ
By Male, Edward
ISBN 13: 978-1-60608-679-7
Publication date 4/23/2009
Previously published by Skeffington & Son, 1891

TALIBUS POST APOSTOLOS, SANCTA ECCLESIA PLANTATORIBUS,

RIGATORIBUS, EDIFICATORIBUS PASTORIBUS, NUTRITORIBUS,

CREVIT (*St. Augustine, contra Julianum, Lib. iii., Cap. iv., No.* 37).

# CONTENTS.

Translator's Preface.

List of Fathers cited, with their dates.

## BOOK I.

## 𝔒n the 𝔒ffice and 𝔠haracter of the 𝔓riesthood.

### SECTION I.

ON THE EXCELLENCE AND HOLINESS OF THE PRIESTLY OFFICE.

## SECTION II.

### THE VIRTUES PROPER TO THE CLERICAL ORDER, SEPARATELY CONSIDERED.

---

## BOOK II.

# On the Pastoral Care.

### SECTION I.

#### ON THE BURDEN OF THE PASTORAL CHARGE.

## SECTION II.

### ON THE DUTIES OF PASTORS TOWARDS GOD AND TOWARDS MAN.

## SECTION III.

### ON THE DUTY OF THE PASTOR TOWARDS HIMSELF.

### CONCLUSION AND PRAYER.

# TRANSLATOR'S PREFACE.

In publishing the following pages on the Priesthood the translator has considerably abridged the original work, thus avoiding some needless repetition, and reducing the book to more convenient dimensions. It is his one hope that it may set before its readers, as it is so eminently designed to do, the *unanimous* sentiments of the Church Catholic on its important subject, to the edification both of Priests and people. He need say no more, but he cannot conclude this short Preface without expressing his grateful thanks to the Rev. Canon Paget, the present Professor of Pastoral Theology in the University of Oxford, for his kind assistance and suggestions, especially in the earlier portion of the work, as also to his predecessor, the Lord Bishop of Lincoln, for his lordship's kind permission to dedicate the work to him. He has also to thank the Principals of the Theological Colleges of Cuddesden and Ely for the expression of their general approval of the work, and the Rev. John Keble, of Perry Barr, for his perusal and suggestions.

For the correctness or otherwise of the translation no one is responsible but *himself.* The Latin quotation from St. Augustine, given in the original work, and following the title page, he considers to be its sufficient apology.

EDWARD MALE.

# LIST OF THE FATHERS CITED IN THIS WORK, WITH THE DATES OF THEIR DEATHS.

# Book I.

# On the Office and Character of the Priesthood.

## SECTION I.

### ON THE EXCELLENCE AND HOLINESS OF THE PRIESTLY OFFICE.

### CHAPTER I.

#### ON THE ENGAGEMENT, AND ON THE PORTION OF THE ECCLESIASTIC.

I. A CLERK, who is the servant of the Church of Christ (St. Jerome ad Nepotianum. 5), should begin by reflecting carefully on the signification of this title; and, when its definition has been clearly made out and set before him, strive to *be* what he finds himself to be thereby *called*.

For seeing that the word, κλῆρος, from which it is derived, signifies a lot or portion, it will follow that the Clergy are so called, either because they are themselves the Lord's portion, or because the Lord is theirs. But, whichever of these may be the true interpretation of the word as applied to them, the man who is the Lord's portion, and the man who has the Lord for his portion, are alike bound to exhibit such a character as

shall entitle them either to have the Lord for their
portion or to be possessed by the Lord as His.   When
a man possesses the Lord, and can say with the
Prophet, "The Lord is my portion" (Ps. xvi. 6), there
must be nothing else that he can call his portion but
the Lord.   If he possess (as his *portion*) anything else
but the Lord, he ceases to have the Lord for his
portion.   If he have gold or silver, for example, or
lands, or furniture (setting store by them as his "portion"), the Lord will not stoop to be classed with such
possessions as these as his portion.   If, on the other
hand, I am myself the Lord's portion and "the lot of
His inheritance" (Deut. xxxii. 9), I cease to have any
part among the other tribes, and, like the Priest and
the Levite of old, I live on the tithes, and by serving
at the Altar am made partaker of the offerings thereon.
"Having food and raiment, therewith I am content"
(1 Tim. vi. 8), and naked myself I follow the naked
Cross of my Lord.

2. But how few are the men (St. Ambrose on Ps. cxix.
Serm. 8) in this world of ours, who are able to *say*,
"The Lord is my portion"?   What a stranger to
vice must such an one be!   How far removed from
every stain of sin, whose heart is thus detached from
every thing that concerns this life, and clings to nothing
that is of this world!   The avaricious man cannot say,
"The Lord is my portion," for Avarice will step forward
and say, "It is to me that you belong, not the Lord.
It is I that have brought you into bondage; I that
you have served; I to whom you sold yourself in that

gold yonder ; I to whom you assigned yourself in such and such landed property." The luxurious man cannot say it ; for luxury will step forward and say, " I am thy portion ; I made a slave of you in that feast which you will remember ; I caught you in the net of that banquet of delicacies, and I hold you bound to me by the testimony of your greed. Have you forgotten that your table was dearer to you than life itself ? I appeal to your own conscience, deny it if you can ; but you cannot." Neither can the adulterer say, " The Lord is my portion," for voluptuousness will step forward and say, " It is I who am your portion. At such a time you fell under my authority and under my juris-diction." The traitor cannot say it, for at once the baseness of his offence will rush in and say, " He lies to Thee, Lord Jesus ; he is mine." We have an instance to the point ; for when Judas had received the " sop " from Christ, the Devil entered into his heart, claiming, as it were, his possession ; laying hold on the right of his portion and saying, as it were, by this action, " This man is not Thine, but mine. My servant certainly, but Thy betrayer. Mine he is past all question, not Thine. He sits at table indeed with Thee, but he serves me. He feasts indeed with Thee, but he feeds with me. He has received bread from Thee—from me, money. He drinks wine with Thee, but has sold Thy very blood to me." And how truly he had, in effect, thus spoken, he at once gave proof ; for Christ at once withdrew Himself from Judas ; and Judas also left Jesus, and followed the Devil.

3. Would you furthermore understand (Eucherius, on Gen. xlvii. 22) the difference between the priests of God and the priests of Pharaoh? Pharaoh gave land to his priests. God gave no such inheritance to His. "I," He saith, "am your portion " (Numbers xviii. 20). Consider, then, my readers, and all ye priests of the Lord, and observe these distinctions; lest those who have their portion in this world, and spend their time in mere worldly studies and pursuits, should appear to be not so much priests of the Lord as priests of Pharaoh. " Except a man forsake all that he hath," saith the Lord, " he cannot be My disciple " (Luke xiv. 33).

I tremble as I repeat these words: Jesus Christ repudiates as His true disciple the man to whom He perceives that anything still belongs as his *portion*— the man who has not forsaken, as his *portion*, all that he possessed. What then shall we do? How shall we read these words ourselves or repeat them to the people, if we have not only neglected to renounce our possessions, but are ready to acquire others that we never had, before coming to Christ? *

4. Jesus Christ, then, is your inheritance, O ye ministers of the Lord! (Amb. in Ps. cxix. 8, 7). Jesus Christ is your sole domain. His Name is your wealth,

---

* This language will seem extreme; but it may be practically interpreted, in the case of clergy who have private property, that they should regard it as consecrated with themselves to the service of God, and enabling them to assist impoverished Churches at their own cost, or, in the case of married clergy, meet family claims—so often, as we too well know, a serious strain upon many a poorly endowed parish priest.

His Name your income, His Name constitutes your stipend—a stipend, not of money but of grace. Your heritage is not dried up by heat, nor devastated by storm. " The sun shall not burn thee by day, neither the moon by night" (Ps. cxxi. 6). Keep, then, the portion which you have chosen, for it is "the good portion," which the possessions of this world cannot equal.

5. Let your orators treasure up their learning (St. Paulinus ad Aprum. 6), your philosophers their wisdom, your rich men their riches, your kings their dominions! To *us* Jesus Christ alone is glory, fortune, empire, everything. Let other men choose alike such portions as they prefer (St. Aug. in Ps. xvi. 5), earthly and temporal; the portion of the Saints is the Everlasting Lord. Let others enjoy their draught of deadly pleasures;—" The Lord is the portion of my inheritance, and of my Cup."

# CHAPTER II.

## *THAT NO MAN SHOULD JOIN THE CLERICAL ORDER WITHOUT CLEARLY RECOGNIZING THE PROPER DISPOSITIONS IN HIMSELF, AND THE WILL OF GOD.*

1. IT is a difficult and arduous task to discharge the functions of the Priesthood (Peter Blois, Ep. 123 ad Ricard. Episc. Lond :, and Greg. de cur. past. iii. 4), to guide souls, and, as Solomon saith, " to put himself at the head of the people, and thus burden himself with a double weight of sins " (Ecclus. vii. 6-8. See also iii. 18). The Lord hath said it :—" If any of My Priests, after having received the Holy Unction, shall have fallen into sin, he maketh My people to sin also" (Leviticus iv. 3. Vulg :). On which passage the blessed Gregory makes this remark :—" The Priests should know that, if they commit errors, they are worthy of as many deaths as they transmit to their flocks examples of their own transgressions." And who is there that is fully acquainted with his own works ? Who that knoweth for certain whether he be an object of love or of hatred ? Who that knoweth, as he ought to know, his own faults ? " The heart is deceitful above all things and desperately

wicked; who can know it?" (Jer. xvii. 9). A profound abyss, indeed, dark and unsearchable, is the conscience of the sinner.

2. "As My Father hath sent Me, even so send I you." By these words (St. Cyril Alex. on John xx. 20, 21) our Lord Jesus Christ ordained the guides and teachers of the world, and the dispensers of His Divine Mysteries, whom He commands to shine as lights in the world, and to enlighten with their doctrine the entire race of man scattered over the face of the whole world. With good truth, therefore, does St. Paul speak, when he says that no one should take upon himself that honour "but he that is called of God" (Hebrews v. 4). (Compare the first question put to Priests and Deacons in our ordination service. Ed.)

3. Hear ye the Lord's complaint (St. Bern. de Colloq: Simonis cum Jesu, 45 (apoc) ). "They have reigned," He saith, "but not by Me; they have set up princes, but I knew them not" (Hos. viii. 4). Of a surety in the case of all those in ecclesiastical orders, and in other offices pertaining to the Sanctuary, who seek therein their own honour, or wealth, or pleasure, or, in a word, are *their own* and not Jesus Christ's (Phil. i. 21), it is at once and undoubtedly manifest that it has not been that Love (*Caritas*), which is God, that has led them to their position, but that which is wholly alien to God, and is "the root of all evil," namely, cupidity. What rashness! nay, what madness! Where is the fear of God in such cases? Where the recollection of death? Where the dread of hell and that "fearful

looking for of the day of judgment" which is meet
(Heb. x. 27)?   The Bride will not intrude herself into
the bed, or even into the private chamber of the king,
except by his permission (Cant. ii. 4); but thou rudely
enterest into it without either invitation or introduction.
"Draw me, and we will run after Thee," saith that
chaste Spouse; "We will run after the odour of Thy
perfumes" (Cant. i. 4).   But now every man is led by
his own pleasure (—"Trahit sua quemque voluptas;"
Virg. Eclog. ii. 65) and following the scent of sordid
gain, they esteem godliness as a mere source of income
(1 Tim. vi. 5); "whose damnation is just" (Rom. iii. 8).

"Thou castest them down as they were being raised
up;" saith the Prophet (Ps. lxxiii. 18, cf. vulg.).   He
saith not, "Thou hast cast them down *after* Thou hadst
raised them up; but whilst they were *being* raised up."
For there are some who, being evilly disposed and
puffed up with temporal honours, while seeming to
others to be rising, are inwardly falling downwards.
Their very elevation is their downfall.   Hence it is
said again:—"They shall consume away like *smoke*"
(Ps. xxxvii. 20).   For it is by ascending into the air
that smoke consumes away.   It is in spreading itself
out that it is dissipated.   So is it also with the sinner,
when good fortune attends him in this life; for the
very circumstances which exhibit him to others as
rising, are the cause of his own utter downfall.

# CHAPTER III.

---

*THAT THE UNDERTAKING OF THE OFFICE OF THE
PRIESTHOOD SHOULD BE PRECEDED BY A
CONFIRMED COURSE OF VIRTUE.*

---

1. THE Prophet Moses (Peter Blois, Ep. 123 ad
Ric : Episc. Londin :), when chosen to be
the leader of his people and about to be
sent to Pharaoh, and, in like manner, Jeremiah also,
on being called of God to instruct His rebellious people,
humbly excused themselves ; but unquestionably the
Sacerdotal dignity is as superior to the office of the
Ancient Prophet as the reality is to the anticipation, or
as the substance is to the shadow, or as the revelation
of the Truth is to its antecedent promises. Nevertheless, even when Isaiah of old offered himself to God for
the ministry of preaching on His demanding whom He
should send, he had first to be cleansed by the coal
taken from the Altar ; for no one is truly qualified for
spiritual ministrations until he is purified by the fire of
the Holy Ghost. He must first be cleansed (Greg.
Naz. Orat : 2 de Sacerdotio.), then cleanse ; first be
built up in wisdom, then build up others ; first be made
a shining light, then illuminate others ; first draw near
to God, then draw others to Him ; first be sanctified,
then sanctify.

2. When the Apostle Paul (Greg. Mag. Ep. 53 ad Virg. Episc. lib. v. ind. 13) forbids a novice to be a candidate for Holy Orders (1 Tim. iii. 6), we are to understand that, as a man was then so called who had been only recently *(noviter)* admitted to the faith, so in our own time we account those to be novices, who have only recently adopted a life of holy conversation. We know that, when walls have just been built, they are not allowed to receive the weight of the beams that are to support the roof, until they have been first permitted to become thoroughly dry of the moisture which has attended them during their construction, lest, receiving their weight before they have become duly solidified, they bring the whole fabric to the ground. In like manner when we cut down young trees for building purposes, we reckon upon the moisture which is due to their greenness being first dried out, lest, if the weight of a building be laid upon them while they are still fresh, they become bent by reason of their very freshness ; and so, proving that they have been elevated to their position too soon, give way the more rapidly. Why then, I would ask, is not this rule observed in the concerns of men, while so much importance is attached to it in matters of wood and stone ?

3. I do not mean to say (St. Bern. de mor. et off. Episc. vii. 26) that a man may be too young for the grace of God.   Certainly not ; any more than he may be too old ; for we see many who are young surpassing their seniors in intelligence, superior to their age in manners, in advance of their years in merit, and mak-

ing up for defect of age by superiority of virtue. They are good youths, who study to be as backward in wickedness as they are in age—in wickedness, I say, not in understanding—and whose youth, as the Apostle counsels us, "no man should despise" (1 Tim. iv. 12). Samuel was a good child, who was a ready listener to the voice of God, and said, "Speak, Lord, for Thy servant heareth" (1 Kings iii. 10); as though he would say: "I made haste and prolonged not the time to keep Thy righteous judgments" (Ps. cxix. 60). A good man, too, was Jeremiah, who, being sanctified from his mother's womb, on his excusing himself on account of his youth, was set nevertheless "over nations and kingdoms" (Jer. i. 6 and 10). Another good man, too, was Daniel, whose spirit the Lord stirred up to expose unjust judgments, and spare the innocent blood (Hist. Susan). In short, "Wisdom is the grey hair unto men, and an unspotted life is old age" (Wisd. iv. 9).

# CHAPTER IV.

## ON THE GREATNESS OF THE POWER WHICH THE PRIESTHOOD POSSESSES OF BINDING AND LOOSING.

I. IT is then to men (Chrys. de Sac. iii. 5)—it is to the inhabitants of the earth, that this power has been given of dispensing the treasures of Heaven. It is to them that there has been entrusted a power, which God, notwithstanding His goodness, has not been willing to grant either to Angels or to Archangels; for at no time did He ever say to those happy spirits, "Whatsoever ye shall bind on earth shall be bound in Heaven; and whatsoever ye shall loose on earth shall be loosed in Heaven."

The Princes of this world have indeed the power to bind, but they can only bind the body; whereas the power of the Priesthood extends to the soul, and penetrates even into Heaven itself; for whatever be the nature of the sentence which His minister pronounces here below, God ratifies it above and confirms it by His Sovereign authority; and what else is this but to concede to them a power over all celestial things. For "Whosoever sins ye remit," He saith, "they are remitted unto them, and whosoever sins ye retain, they are retained." What power, I would ask, could possibly be greater than this? The Father commits all judgment unto the Son ; but I behold even that very judgment itself handed on by the Son of God to them. It is as though they were already translated into Heaven itself, and placed above the level of all human nature, and delivered from all affections belonging to ourselves, that they are thus conducted to this exalted position. Why, if any *earthly* king were to confer such an honour as this upon any one of his subjects, that he might cast any one he thought fit into prison, and when he pleased release him, such a man would be deemed happy, and worthy of respect and admiration in the judgment of all ; and yet the man who has received an authority from God Himself, as much greater than this as Heaven is more precious than earth, and as the souls of men are more precious than their bodies, this man, I say, would seem to be regarded by some in our day as having received a dignity rather of an inferior character than otherwise. And so much is this the case that it is even possible to find some even of those very persons themselves to whom these grave responsibilities have been entrusted by God, in whose eyes their very own office is contemptible, and who make light of the gift conferred upon them. Away, I say, with such infatuation ! For infatuation assuredly it is, beyond all dispute, to despise so exalted an office as this—an office without which we were incapable of receiving spiritual health, or any of the blessed promises made to us.*

---

* It must be assumed, we suppose, in connection with these passages that the writer takes for granted the *justice* of the Priestly acts referred to, and does not commit the Supreme Judge to a compulsory submission to what may have been an unjust sacerdotal act ; but the passages are none the less salutary and instructive to the Clergy, if this qualification be taken as implied. Ed.

# CHAPTER V.

## ON THE EXCELLENCE AND EFFICACY OF THE DIVINE SACRIFICE.

1. TERRIBLE indeed (Chrys. de Sac. iii. 3) and awe-inspiring were the solemnities of the olden time which preceded the day of grace; such as the golden bells, the pomegranates, the precious stones on the breast of the Priest, and others besides placed upon the shoulders, the mitre, the crown of gold, the robe hanging down to the feet, the golden plates, the Holy of Holies, and the awful silence and repose within! But when we come to look into those things which the day of grace has brought us, we shall regard the fearful and awe-inspiring ordinances of which I have just spoken as mere trifles, and shall perceive that, as Paul saith concerning the Law, now that the Truth itself is come, "even that which was made glorious had no glory in this respect, by reason of the glory which excelleth" (2 Cor. iii. 10). In fact, when we behold the Lord Himself immolated and lying upon the Altar, the Priest engaged in the Sacrifice and in offering up the Prayers, and then the people sprinkled with that Precious Blood and dyed as it were in its Sacred purple, can we regard ourselves as engaged

among mortal men only, and as standing on this lower earth? Are you not rather transported into Heaven itself? Will you not rather cast aside all thought of the flesh, and behold with a naked mind and with a pure soul the things that are in Heaven itself? O the miracle! O the loving-kindness of God! He Who sitteth on high with the Father, is at the same moment handled by the very hands of all, and delivers Himself to be received and embraced by willing souls!

2. But if you would see the excellence of this Consecration in the light of another miracle, to which it may be compared, set before your eyes the prophet Elijah, and that vast multitude gathered around him, and the sacrifice all prepared upon the altar of stones; then the perfect quietness and silence reigning among them all, while the Prophet, all alone, pours forth his prayer, and then the fire all on a sudden descending from Heaven and licking up the sacrifice which was upon the altar! Surely these things are wonderful and full of awe-inspiring marvels! Then let your thoughts pass on from these holy things to the still holier ones which *we* are invited to behold, and you will not perceive them to be merely wonderful, but as surpassing everything else in amazement. For here stands the Priest, not dealing with mere fire, but with the Holy Spirit of God. He pours forth long prayers, not that fire may come down from Heaven and consume the Sacrifice, but that Divine Grace may flow forth upon the Sacrifice, and inflame by its means the minds of all, and make them purer than silver that has been melted in

B

fire, and purified of its dross thereby. This mystery, therefore, so worthy to be held in the deepest reverence, as exceeding all others in greatness, who is there that would not be accounted insane in the very highest degree, and to have been deprived of all natural powers, that should disdain it and hold it in contempt ?

3. Seeing then (Chrys. de Sac. vi. 4), that, when the Priest has invoked the Holy Spirit, and has perfected the sacrifice so worthy of all holy fear and trembling, the Divine Lord of all is devoutly handled by his hands, I would ask you in what rank we should place him, and what purity we should demand from him, and what piety ? Bethink you what hands *they* should be that are engaged to minister in such matters as these, what lips that should utter such words ; in what respect, in short, it is meet that that soul should be more pure and more holy than those of ordinary men, that has received so exalted and so honourable a consecration ! During all that time the Holy Angels stand around the Priest, and the whole order of celestial Powers raise their voices, and the entire vicinity of the Altar is filled with the Chorus of Angels in honour of Him Who is there offered. To believe this, indeed, it suffices only to consider the greatness of the Mystery which is at this time fulfilled. But it has been related to me concerning a certain person of noted piety, and frequently favoured with divine revelations, that he had stated that at the celebration of this Sacrament he was himself favoured with such a vision ;—that he saw, as clearly as human sight could bear it, a multitude of the

heavenly host, clothed in white garments, standing about the Altar and reverently bowing their heads as one would see a guard of soldiers do in the presence of the Sovereign. And, for my part, I find no difficulty in believing it.

# CHAPTER VI.

*THAT WE SHOULD NEVER APPROACH THE ALTAR*
*WITHOUT AROUSING WITHIN OUR BREASTS*
*SENTIMENTS OF PIETY BY THE REMEM-*
*BRANCE OF OUR LORD.*

1. AT the Sacrifice of the Altar there is required of us (Peter Blois, Serm. 56) an especially devout and fervent sense of loving affection for the august Sacrifice we are about to offer ; for in it is comprehended the sum total of our salvation. Unquestionably that Priest is most deficient in devotion, whose spirit is not affected with contrition, when standing at the Altar where the Son of the Most High God is offered up before the Eyes of His Father. As unquestionably, too, will every devout and considerate Priest, when standing at the most Holy Table, think of nothing but of "Jesus Christ and Him crucified," and set before the eyes of his heart His humility and His patience. Devoutly and earnestly will he contemplate His sufferings and His griefs—His reproaches, His spittings, His scourgings, the spear of the soldier, the cross itself and the moment of His death ; and then, as it were, crucify himself in this very recollection of the Passion of his Lord, and offer himself a spiritual

sacrifice to Him and for His sake, Who gave Himself in the flesh a perfect and sufficient Sacrifice for us.

A Priest of the Lord Jesus Christ should be partaker with Him in all the feelings of His Heart and Mind (Peter Blois, Ep. 123 ad Episc. Lond :) ; and *that*, not only so as wholly to empty himself (cf. Phil. ii. 7) by the grace of humility, but that, as representing in himself the crucifixion of the Lord, he should bear in his body the marks of the Lord Jesus, and crucify himself unto the Lord on the Altar of His Cross (Gal. vi. 7 and ii. 20). It is one of the sayings of Solomon, " When thou sittest to eat with a ruler, consider diligently what is before thee " (Prov. xxiii. 1). Under the Levitical law the Priest retains the skin of the victim, to indicate that, whenever the Priest of the new law should offer the salutary Sacrifice on the Table of the Altar, he should put himself into harmony with the Divine Victim by the cross of compunction.

2. We read in the Epistles of S. Paul, " Let a man examine himself, and so let him eat of that Bread and drink of that Cup " (1 Cor. xi. 28). Happy is the man who is found so to have examined himself. " Examine me, O Lord, and prove me ; try out my reins and my heart " (Ps. xxvi. 2), that I may be meet to partake of so great a Sacrament ! For fearful are the words that follow :—" He that eateth the Flesh of Christ and drinketh His Blood unworthily, eateth and drinketh damnation to himself " (1 Cor. xi. 29).

It is clear why it is said that they have no power to partake of the celestial Altar, who serve the tabernacle

(Hebr. xiii. 10) ; for to those who are given up to fleshly lusts the Cup of the Lord is turned into the "poison of dragons" (Deut. xxxii. 33). The Bread of Angels is withheld from such ; the celestial Manna has become putrefied to them. It is to be noted that it is by the same sun that fleshly substances are hardened, and manna is melted (Ex. xvi. 21) ; teaching us that according to men's different deserts God permits some to be hardened in their malice, and lets others be melted into saving tears by a religious devotion ; and while the former, as by a feeble and fastidious stomach, receive, as it were, but the bran and rind of the Sacrament, the souls of the latter fatten upon the celestial Food and the inner marrow of the Divine corn (cf. Deut. xxxii. 14). The spirit of the one is like "the mountain of Gilboa," upon which "neither dew nor rain falleth" (2 Kings i. 21), while, in the case of the other, God "hath sent a gracious rain upon His inheritance" (Ps. lxviii. 9).

3. It is necessary, then, that when we offer the Sacrifice to God (Greg. Mag. Dial. lib. 4. c. 59), we should at the same time sacrifice ourselves to God in our hearts by due contrition, seeing that we who celebrate the Mysteries of the Divine Passion, ought to imitate in ourselves what we do Sacramentally. For it will only then be in the most perfect truth a Sacrifice for us, when we at the same time offer up ourselves also as a sacrifice.* But it must be our studious aim that, even after the hour of prayer is passed, we should, to the

---

* Compare Post-Communion Prayer in the English Office. Ed.

utmost extent of the ability which God hath given us, keep our souls in Him as the sole source of our spiritual strength and vigour, lest our thoughts wander away when our task is over, lest a mere empty joy take possession of our minds, and our soul lose all the benefit of its contrition by an unguarded licence of spirit.

(Two chapters of the original work are here omitted for brevity's sake, as being largely a repetition of the same thoughts from Tertullian, Prosper, Basil, and Peter Blois.)

# CHAPTER VII.

### ON THE EXCELLENCE OF PSALMODY AND OF THE DIVINE OFFICE; AND ON THE DEVOTION WITH WHICH IT SHOULD BE ENGAGED IN.

1. PRIESTS have sundry functions to discharge (Pet. Blois, Serm. in Syn. 56. " Ignis semper ardebit "). They receive confessions; they baptize, and they preach the Word; but Psalmody and the celebration of the Holy Sacrifice are also their special concern, and both alike require on their part an humble and fervent piety.

Of what use, one may well ask, is the chanting of the Psalms, if there be no true piety in the heart? To sing without devotion is like sounding brass and a tinkling cymbal (1 Cor. xiii. 1). It is not with the lips only, but from the heart that we must pray to God. It were better to sing five Psalms with purity of soul, and with recollection and spiritual fervour, than the whole Psalter with a troubled and distracted mind (St. Jerome, Reg. Monach. c. xiv. Apoc.). If the Psalmist prays, pray thou with him. If he mourns, mourn with him. If he rejoices, rejoice with him. Hope with his hope, and tremble with his fear.

All the members of the Saviour united to their head

(Aug. on Ps. lx.), and bound together with the cords of charity and peace, constitute, as it were, but one person ; and their united voices are heard in the Psalms as one voice, and whatever is written in them is as a mirror of one's self.

2. "*All* scripture," in fact (St. Athanas. ad Marcellinum), whether of the Old Testament or of the New, " is given by the inspiration of God, and is profitable for doctrine, for reproof, for correction, for instruction in righteousness " )1 Tim. iii. 16), in that particular form of words in which it was originally conceived ; but the Book of *Psalms* demands our especial attention and close observation. Each separate Book indeed of Holy Scripture supplies us with its own proper information ; but the Book of Psalms, like a garden in which every kind of tree is planted, by combining and uniting all the rest, displays, as we sing them, the peculiar beauties of the whole. Not only is the whole of Scripture there, in a manner, reproduced ; but every man can study by means of them the sentiments of his own heart, and find a form in which he can best express his personal feelings, and *that* in the language best adapted to his soul's condition. In reading other parts of Scripture it is obvious that what he is reading is no *personal* concern of his, but only that of the holy men of whom it is written. In the Psalms, on the contrary, it is their peculiar beauty that each person who reads them, (the prophecies concerning Christ and the Gentiles alone excepted) believes that he finds in them the best expression of his own heart under the circumstances of

his own private life ; so much so that he recites them
as though they had been specially composed for himself.
I conceive, indeed, that there is to be found in the
Book of Psalms a complete picture of the life of man.
All the affections of his heart, and all the interior
thoughts of his mind are here expressed in the language
and in the spirit which best suits them, neither can anything be found in human affairs which is not more or
less touched upon in them.

3. Let your mode of chanting, then (St. Bernard, Ep.
398 ad Guid. Abb. 2), be characterized by gravity :—
neither effeminate nor too coarse or hurried. Let it
be pleasing, but not with levity ; so reaching the ear as
to affect the heart. Let it be such as shall dispel
sorrow, subdue anger, and give force to the words
rather than obscure them. Carelessness in chanting
does not promote grace ; and even when we are over-
particular about the musical rendering, we destroy the
moral effect of the words.

" Let all those that seek Thee rejoice and be glad in
Thee, and let all such as delight in Thy salvation say
alway, the Lord be praised " (Ps. lxx. 4). But *they* do
not love His salvation who jumble and cut short the
words of the office, and God has no pleasure in such
inarticulate praises. Speaking of Psalmody, St. Jerome
says that a man should join real prayer with the words
he utters. Two things, therefore, are necessary for
good chanting, viz. : the attention of the mind and the
devotion of the heart. To such chanting as this the
Angels, yea, and the Lord of the Angels Himself, draw

near.   They take pleasure in joining with us, and we see fulfilled the words of the Prophet, " Unto Thee, O Lord, will I sing ; O let me have understanding in the way of godliness."  And what saith the Apostle to the same purpose ?   " I would rather utter five words with my understanding, than ten thousand in an unknown tongue " (1 Cor. xiv. 9).

## CHAPTER VIII.

*THAT THE SANCTITY OF THE PRIEST OUGHT NOT TO BE LESS THAN THE DIGNITY OF HIS OFFICE.*

1. HAVE you been honoured, my brother (St. Ephraim de Sac. iii. 4), with the dignity of the Priesthood, be studious to please Him Who hath conferred that great honour upon you, that so you may prove to be to Him a true soldier in chastity and righteousness, and in divine wisdom, and in conspicuous purity of life. Inflame your soul with a holy fervour. Be temperate as Joseph; chaste as Joshua; hospitable as Abraham; a lover of poverty as Job; as merciful as David, and as meek as Moses. Bring back the erring; strengthen the lame; help the infirm, and the like.

2. The office of the Priesthood is discharged on earth (St. Chrys. de Sac. iii. 4), but it is to be referred to the class and order of things heavenly. And how justly so! It was no mere mortal being, no Angel either, nor Archangel, nor any created power whatever, but the Holy Spirit Himself Who instituted it, and Who has entrusted to weak mortals, still abiding in this corruptible flesh, this angelic ministry. Consequently it is of necessity that the priest should be as pure as if

he stood in the very midst of those celestial spirits
*(virtutes)*.

3. And now listen to my song (St. Bernard, de Consid.
lib. 2. c. 7. 14)—less sweet indeed than hitherto, but
salutary! Surely a monstrous thing is a high dignity
coupled with a degraded soul—a lofty station with a
debased life—a tongue uttering great words, and hands
engaged in hateful deeds—many words and no fruits—
vast authority and no stability! For what else is
authority without loftiness of merit, but an honourable
title without the man? (Salvian adv. avarit. ii. 9, and
de Gub. Dei. iv. 1). Or what is a dignity in the hands
of one unworthy of it, but an ornament set in clay?
All therefore who are raised to a position in the Sacred
Orders, should excel in virtue in proportion as they are
thus elevated in rank.

# CHAPTER IX.

*AN EXHORTATION TO PRIESTS TO MAKE WORTHY*
*USE OF SO DIGNIFIED AN OFFICE.*

1. HOW high a dignity has God conferred upon you (St. Bern. Serm. in Synod. 1. Apoc.)! How great are the prerogatives of your order! God has set you in spiritual things above Kings and Emperors. He has preferred your order above all other orders whatsoever. Nay, to speak yet more boldly, He has set you above Angels and Archangels, above Thrones and Dominions. For, as He took not upon Himself the nature of Angels but the seed of Abraham, in order to accomplish our redemption (Hebr. ii. 16), so He entrusted His sacred Body and Blood to the Priests alone. For, saith the Apostle, "Are they not all ministering spirits" (that is, the Angels) "sent forth to minister for them who shall be heirs of Salvation" (Hebr. i. 14)?

2. We have beheld (St. Ambrose in Ps. xxxviii.) the Prince of Priests coming to us; we have beheld Him and heard His Voice, offering His blood for us. We, His Priests, follow Him, in so far as we are able, that we may offer the Sacrifice on behalf of the people (Hebr. v. 3). Feeble, indeed, are we, as regards any

merit of our own, but honourable by virtue of the Sacrifice which we offer; for albeit Christ Himself is not now visible to the eye, offering Himself to God for us, yet He is virtually offered on our behalf here below, when the Body of Christ is offered; nay, He Himself is made manifest as offering Himself in us, Whose word it is which sanctifies the offering made by us.

O ye Priests of the Lord (Aug. Serm. 7 ad fratres in eremo (apoc.)), if the soul of every righteous man is the abode of God, much more ought ye to be His abode, and His pure and spotless temple. If His tomb was glorious on which His dead Body rested (Isaiah xi. 10), how much more glorious and more worthy should your bodies be, in which He daily condescends to take up His abode, now that He is risen from the dead! If the womb was blessed which bare Christ within it for the space of nine months, how blessed must your hearts be which the Son of God daily elects to make His dwelling-place! If blessed are the paps which, as a little child, He sucked, how blessed must that mouth be which receives His Flesh and drinks His Blood! Let your flesh therefore "tremble with fear" (Psalm cxix. 120), and see to yourselves that the tongue which calls down the Son of God from Heaven, speak not a word against God, and that the hands which are stained with the Blood of Christ be not polluted by sin.

3. That it is to a lofty eminence of sanctity (Hildebert, Serm. 97) that the Priest is called, we are led to believe from the words of the Prophet, where he says:—" O Zion that bringest good tidings, get up into the high

mountain " (Is. xl. 9). " Get up," he says, "into the high mountain." Moses went up into a high mountain to receive the law of the Lord (Ex. xix. 20). St. Luke tells us that, when Mary had conceived in her womb the Son of God, she " went into the hill country with haste " (i. 39). Christ also was wont to pray upon the mountains (Matt. xiv. 23), and was transfigured on a mountain (Matt. xvii. 2) ; and, although, as Pope Leo saith (Serm. iv. de Pass. Dom.), many another mode of death would have served His purpose for our redemption, nevertheless He chose the *elevation* of the Cross. In all these instances it is clearly pointed out that the life of the Priest should be *lofty* in its aspirations, seeing that he is the teacher of the law for the people of the Lord, who undertakes to pray for sinners, " and to be made all things to all men, that he may by all means save some " (1 Cor. ix. 22).

It is a crime surely for one that is set apart for such an office as this to be attached to earthly things. It is the will of God that the Minister of the Altar should be on a level with *(similis)* his ministry, and that the man who is consecrated to lofty duties should exhibit a corresponding sanctity of character. It is His will that he should " walk in the Spirit," to whose office He has subjected the unclean spirits (Luke xx. 17) ; and He desires, lastly, that he should become a pure and a clean vessel, seeing that it is said by the Prophet concerning the Priest, " Be ye clean that bear the vessels of the Lord " (Is. lii. 11). But they that " bear the *vessels of the Lord* " are the Priests ; who, by the discharge of their sacerdotal ministry, introduce *faithful souls* into the tabernacle of Heaven.   Hence it is necessary that they who thus " bear the vessels of the Lord" should become as vessels of the Lord themselves ; not vessels of earth, but of gold ; not for contempt, but for honour; not such as Belshazzar shall drink out of with his wives and concubines, but out of which the Redeemer shall " drink with His disciples of the fruit of the True Vine in the Kingdom of His Father"—that is to say, not vessels which the Devil shall delight in with those whom he has brought into subjection to every kind of vice, and whom he makes use of for every kind of iniquity ; but vessels in which He Who saith to His disciples, " I am the Vine and ye are the Branches," may drink with them of the fruit of the Vine ; that is to say, that He may rejoice and exult in the effusion of His own Blood, by Which He has purchased to Himself vessels so precious.

---

C

# CHAPTER X.

1. I WOULD have thee (St. Bernard de Consideratione, lib. 2. ch. vii. 14) strive after the highest degree of perfection, and not to fancy, or to have it fancied for thee by others, that thou hast attained to it already, when thou hast not done so ; else how shalt thou make any progress therein, if thou art already satisfied with thy condition ? Let it not therefore be your habit to be slow in detecting your faults, or to be ashamed of acknowledging them when detected. Let your language be like that of the Apostle—" Not that I have already attained, nor that I am already perfect " (Phil. iii. 12) ; and again, " I count not myself to have apprehended " (Ibid 13). Such is the wisdom of the Saints, and it is very different from that which " puffeth up " (1 Cor. viii. 1). The man who seeks after this true wisdom, seeketh sorrow ; but it is a *profitable* sorrow, and one that will be avoided by none that are wise. It is a wholesome sorrow, by which the deadly stupor of the

hard and impenitent soul is dispelled; and hence he was a wise man that was able to say of himself, " My heaviness is ever in my sight" (Ps. xxxviii. 17).

2. Trust not too much (St. Bernard de Consid. i. 2) to your present state of mind and feelings. Nothing ever remains so fixed in the mind that neglect and the course of time will not more or less obliterate it. What will not custom and habit sometimes overthrow? What is there that will not grow hard and cold by the force of habit? What is there that will not give way to use and custom? How many there are to whom things, which for their bitterness they have at first shrunk from, have by use become at last sweet and agreeable. Hear what the righteous man says so lamentingly over such persons! " The things that my soul once refused to touch are become my sorrowful meat," *i.e.*, "my meat in my sorrow" (Job vi. 7). At first something may seem to you utterly unendurable, but in course of time, if you let yourself become accustomed to it, you will not think so much of it. After a while you will think it trifling, then you will not feel it at all, and later on you will come to take delight in it. It is thus that, little by little, men fall into hardness of heart, and from that into utter aversion (for good).

3. Live thou, then (Aug. Ep. ad Sebast. 248, 1), in that state of mind of which it is written, " It grieveth me when I see the transgressors, because they keep not Thy Law " (Ps. cxix. 158). Such a grief as this is a truly religious sentiment, and, if one may so call it, a *happy* sorrow; namely, to be troubled at others' faults

rather than to be implicated in them ; to lament over them, rather than to take part in them ; to be torn with grief because of them, rather than to be drawn into sympathy with them.    Such is the mental persecution which all have to endure who would live religiously in Christ, agreeably to that severe, but true saying of the Apostle—" All that will live godly in Christ Jesus shall suffer persecution " (2 Tim. iii. 12).    For what greater persecution can there be of the life of the good, than the life of the wicked ; not indeed when it constrains them to adopt it, but when it constrains them, on the contrary, to weep at the sight of it.

THE VIRTUES PROPER TO THE CLERICAL ORDER
SEPARATELY CONSIDERED.

## CHAPTER I.

*THE LOVE OF PRAYER, AS ESSENTIALLY NECESSARY
TO THE PRIEST.*

1. NO man ever became perfect all at once. (St. Bernard Serm. i. on St. Andrew, 10). It is by climbing, not by flying, that the top of the ladder is reached. We must ascend it accordingly with the aid of two feet; and these two feet are *meditation* and *prayer*. Meditation reveals to us our need: prayer obtains for us its remedy. The one points the way: the other conducts you along it. By the one we learn the perils which beset our path. By the other we are enabled to escape them.

And in the first place (St. Bernard de consid. i. 7, 8), consideration is necessary to purify the very source of meditation—that is to say, the mind from which it proceeds. Then further it regulates the affections of the soul, directs its actions, corrects its excesses, forms its habits and manners, dignifies and rules its life, and, lastly, imparts to it a correct knowledge of things both human and divine.

We know God (Greg. Mag. on 1 Kings; lib. li. c. iv.
13) by faith in the report we receive of Him; but it is
by the loving contemplation of Him that the man who
has thus heard of Him by the hearing of the ear,
discerns Him, as it were, by a sort of manifestation of
His Presence. Ever so perfect a knowledge of all
things else profits us nothing, except it be crowned by
the knowledge of God. When I see a man (St.
Chrysostom de precatione. Apocr.) not loving the
exercise of prayer, with perseverance, it becomes
evident to me that there can be no excellence in his
soul. The strong and stable soul has its foundation in
religious meditation and prayer (St. Cyprian ad Fortu-
natum, de exhort. martyr. c. 12).

2. "Jesus continued all night in prayer to God"
(Luke vi. 12). Here is an example set for you (St.
Ambrose on Luke v. 43), and a pattern for you to
imitate. For what does it not become you to do for
your own salvation, if Christ on *your* behalf spent the
whole night in prayer? How should *you* behave, when
about to enter upon any special religious function, when
Christ Himself, before sending forth His Apostles, first
prayed, and prayed alone? Resolve in your mind
(Peter Blois, Tract de institut. Episc. c. 4) what advance
you have made since your first assumption of the priestly
rank, and at your daily devotions consider what progress
you have to show in virtue; whether you have become
more humble or more arrogant; more affable or more
austere; more gentle or more harsh; more liberal or
more mean. For, from a certain obligation which

attaches to your office, there is required of you an
increasing measure of spiritual fruit, so that you should
be more earnest in prayer, more studious in reading,
more strictly chaste, more severely sober, more patient
in trials, more restrained in laughter, more amiable in
conversation, more grave in countenance, in gesture,
and in dress ; more controlled in your words, more
given to tears, and more fervent in charity. Render,
then, an account to yourself of your daily actions (cf.
Luke xvi. 2). See each day and night whether you
have passed it without any stain of sin ; whether you
have been negligent in reading or in prayer ; whether
in your words, or in your food and drink, or in the
matter of sleep, you have exceeded the bounds of
temperance ; and know, too, that it is no small loss of
time which you suffer to take place in idleness or in
reading stories.

## CHAPTER II.

*THAT WE SHOULD LEAVE SECULAR MATTERS
TO MEN OF THE WORLD.*

1. IT is written (St. Cyprian, Ep. 66, ad clerum et populum) " No man that warreth entangleth himself with the affairs of this life, that he may please him who hath chosen him to be a soldier" (2 Tim. ii. 4)—a saying which, while applicable to all states of life, is still more so to that of the clergy, who are so strictly charged, as they are, to abstain from all secular and distracting occupations, and, being engaged wholly in things divine and spiritual, not to venture on withdrawing themselves from the Church, or on busying themselves in mere worldly and secular affairs; for their ordination and functions are typified by those of the Levites of the Old Testament, who, when the land was divided, and when their several possessions were assigned to the other eleven tribes, which had no part in the duties of the Temple, or of the Altar, or in any divine ministry whatever, had no share allotted to them in that distribution; but, while it was left to the rest of the tribes to cultivate the land, they alone devoted themselves to the service of God, and received for their support from the remain-

ing eleven tribes the tenth part of the fruits of the earth (Deut. xviii. 1).

Such as this is the present position and *status* of the clergy, namely, that those who are promoted by clerical ordination in the Church of God, should on no account be drawn aside from the discharge of their proper functions, or be tied to secular occupations and cares, but that they should subsist on the tithes of their fellow tribes; in no wise departing from the service of the Altar or from the Sacred Offices, but applying themselves exclusively, night and day, to things heavenly and spiritual.

2. Let not, then, such associations as are foreign to your office so engage your attention that the bottomless pit of secular affairs should swallow up your souls, for which Christ died. Draw around you, continually, a certain interior solitude, that so, being collected within yourself, your mind may not ramble on *(defluat)* to external things, nor be let running on what happens out of doors, or what is bruited abroad. Be alone in a multitude, becoming by this course one of those of whom the blessed Job speaks, where he says, " These are they which built desolate places for themselves ; " " where the wicked cease from troubling, and the weary are at rest " (Job. iii. 14, 17).

## CHAPTER III.

1. SIMON, was of a truth obedient (St. Bernard Colloq. cum Jesu, No. 32. Apocr.), when he accepted his call without any conditions on the hearing of the ear. For at one word of command both he and Andrew "left all, and followed Jesus" (Matt. iv. 20). But, if to the carnal-minded this seems rather to be folly on their part, let him hear what St. Paul says, " The foolishness of God is wiser than men " (1 Cor. i. 25), and again, " It has pleased God through the foolishness of preaching to save them that believe;" because " the world by wisdom knew Him not " (1 Cor. i. 21). For how many has the wisdom (falsely so-called) of this world caused to fall, and has extinguished in them the Spirit which had been conceived in them (1 Thess. v. 19), and which God had desired to have yet more fervently kindled in them. Beware, He seems to say, of acting precipitately. Weigh the matter well in your mind ; examine yourselves more carefully ! It is a great matter which you have set before you, and a work demanding much deliberation.

2. Let the man, therefore, who presumes on his own strength, put himself to the test; for the strength of God is clearly demonstrable. Let him consult his friends, who bears in mind the saying of the prophet, "A man's *enemies* are those of his own household" (Micah vii. 6). Why should a man study the Gospel, if he does not apply it to his own case, and comply with its counsels? And do we not read in it that, when a certain person promising to follow the Lord, asked that he might "first go and bury his *father*," the answer that he received was, "Let the dead bury their dead, but follow thou Me" (Matt. viii. 21, 22)? And again, "No man having put his hand to the plough and looking back is fit for the Kingdom of Heaven" (Luke ix. 62).

# CHAPTER IV.

*CONCERNING ZEAL FOR THE HOUSE OF GOD.*

1. IT is one of the occupations most worthy of the Priesthood (Ambrose de Off. min. ii. 21) to adorn the Temple of God with becoming ornament, so that even with this outward token of honour the House of the Most High shall be glorified. How discreditable it is that some are so indifferent about the furniture of the Sacred Altar (Pet. Damien contra. inscit. cleric. i. 3), and manifest such indifference to it, that they will be content to see chalices of some cheap and inferior metal growing rusty from long neglect, and to cover the Sacred Body of the Lord with soiled linen. What shall I say further about the old rags with which they cover the Altars themselves? What about the Sacred Vessels, so essential to those most holy functions, and about the ornaments appointed for the Priest himself? And what, too, about the sacred books in which one can scarcely decipher even such portions as should be the most deeply engraven in our memories? Matters, all these, which, as soon as noticed, excite ridicule in the minds of those who are disposed to levity, but sadness in all graver spirits.

2. An undoubting faith in God (St. Jerome, Dialog. adv. Lucif. 15) is a grace difficult to find. To take an instance, by way of making my meaning plain. I am engaged in prayer. I should not be so if I had not some sort of faith; but if I had *true* faith I should purify my heart, by which alone it is that God is seen. I should smite upon my breast, I should bedew my cheeks with tears, I should tremble throughout my whole body, I should grow pale and should cast myself down at the feet of my Lord, and wash them with my tears, and wipe them with the hairs of my head. I should assuredly cling to the foot of the Cross, nor let it go till I had obtained mercy (Gen. xxxii. 26). But on the contrary, it more commonly happens that, when I should be praying, I am pacing the cloisters, or counting my gains, or carried away by degrading thoughts, such as I should blush to particularize. Thus it is that I spend the time. What has become of my faith? Do we fancy that the Prophet Jonas prayed thus in the belly of the whale, or the three children in the furnace of fire, or Daniel among the lions, or the thief upon the Cross? Surely not. But let every man consult his own heart, and he will find how rare a thing is a soul so truly faithful that it shall not be influenced more or less by the love of glory, or by the common talk of men. The man who fasts, seldom fasts "as unto the Lord," or, in giving to the poor, gives "as unto the Lord." Vices are the close neighbours of virtues; it is not *easy* to be contented with the sole judgment of God.

3. As we admire the Creator of all things (Jerome,
Ep. 35 ad Hesiod. 12), not in the vast Heavens only,
or in the Earth, or in the Sun, or in the Ocean, or in
Elephants, Camels, Horses, Oxen, Leopards, Bears
and Lions; but also in the lesser and minute animals,
such as ants, butterflies, worms, and such like, of which
we know the forms better than we do the names; and
in all alike we discern and reverence the self-same
creative skill; just so the mind that is devoted to
Christ, is as intent upon the *lesser* as upon the greater
features of his character; knowing that an account is
to be given to Him of every idle word (Matt. xii. 36).
Thus Nepotian was alike diligent that the Altar should
be bright and beautiful, that the walls of the Church
should be kept clean, the pavement bright, the door-
keeper at his post, and the curtains constantly before
the [chancel] doors; that the sanctuary itself also
should be clean, and the vessels bright. Care was
displayed in all the ceremonies of religion, and no
neglect of the Office was suffered. Whenever you
sought for him he was to be found in the Church. He
decorated the tombs of the Martyrs with flowers and
other ornaments, and in all similar respects exemplified
the care and diligence of the Priest.

# CHAPTER V.

1. "WHO shall ascend into the hill of the Lord, or who shall rise up in His Holy Place?" He alone ( St. Bernard, Ep. 393 ad Patriarcham Hierosol. 2 and 3) has the right to ascend thither, who has learned from the Lord Jesus Christ to be "meek and lowly in heart" (Matt. xi. 29). The humble man is alone in a condition to "go up higher," seeing that humility has no lower place *(humus)* that it can descend to. The proud man, albeit he may yet ascend higher, yet cannot long rest there. You, therefore, set, though you be, on high, "be not high-minded, but fear" (Rom. xi. 26), and "humble yourselves under the mighty Hand of God" (1 Pet. v. 6), Who "treads upon the necks of the high and lofty ones" (cf. Deut. xxxiii. 29). Fear (St. Bernard, Ep. 238, No. 4) lest it happen unto thee that thou utter that mournful cry:— "Thou hast taken me up and cast me down" (Ps. cii. 10). A high place is indeed assigned to thee, but not any the safer; a lofty one, but not a secure one. Terrible indeed is that place:—"The place whereon thou standest is holy ground" (Exod. iii. 5).

2. Humility (St. Bernard de off. Episc. Ep. ad Henr.

Abp. of Sens, c. 8) is so absolutely necessary to all
other virtues, that without it they would not seem to
be virtues at all.  For example, in order that the grace
of Chastity may be bestowed on anyone, humility is
necessary, seeing that " God giveth grace unto the
*humble*" (1 Pet. v. 5).  It is this humility, therefore,
which makes room for other virtues.  Those which
have been already enjoyed it preserves ; for " To this
man will I look, saith the Lord, even to him that is
poor and of a contrite spirit, and trembleth at My
Word " (Is. lxvi. 2).  Those virtues, too, which are so
preserved, it also makes perfect; for " My strength
is made perfect in weakness," saith St. Paul ; that is,
in humility.  It wages war against pride, which is the
enemy of all grace and the parent of every kind of sin ;
and it beats off, as well from itself as from all other
virtues of the soul, its haughty tyranny.  While every
other quality of the soul supplies food for this perilous
vice, humility alone makes a stand against its fury ;
and, like an impregnable rampart or citadel, it protects
all the virtues of the soul from its presumptuous
assaults.  And lastly, of all the qualities with which
the soul of Mary was endowed, it is the *only* one to
which she believed that she owed her glorification.
For when the Angel said to her, " Hail, Mary, full of
grace : the Lord is with thee," it seemed that in that
" fulness of grace " which he attributed to her, she
herself recognized none but the grace of humility ; for
her only reply was, " He hath regarded the *lowliness*
of His handmaiden" (Luke i. 48).  What more shall I

say ? Jesus Christ, Who is the Author and Giver of all good gifts, in Whom are hid all the treasures of wisdom and knowledge, and " in Whom dwelleth all the fulness of the Godhead bodily " (Col. ii. 9), did not He, even He, proclaim humility to be the sum and substance of His teaching and of all the virtues which He inculcated ? " Learn of Me," He said, not because I am sober, or chaste, or learned, or anything of that sort, but "because I am meek and lowly in heart " (Luke i. 48). As though He would say, " I send you not to the doctrine of the Fathers, or to the books of the Prophets, but I set Myself before you as a pattern of humility." Both the Angel (Satan) and the woman (Eve) begrudged Me the exalted position which I occupied in the sight of the Father. The Angel envied My Power (Is. xiv. 44) ; the woman My hidden knowledge (Gen. iii. 5). Do ye, then, O ye priests of the Lord, aim rather at a gift more precious than these, and " learn of *Me*," that I am " *meek and lowly in heart* " (cf. 1 Cor. xii. 21).

D

# CHAPTER VI.

## ON THE REMEDY FOR VAIN-GLORY.

1. LET all the progress, then, which you shall make in spiritual exercises *be referred to the praise and glory of Him Who is the King of glory* (Peter Blois, de inst. Episcop). For, of a truth, you are a thief and a robber (John x. 1) if you presume to attribute any such glory to yourself. " Where the rivers rise, thither let them also return " (Eccles. i. 7). " The living creatures," mentioned by Ezekiel, " ran and *returned* " * (Ezek. i. 14). Whatever grace was conferred upon them they attributed to God. " How can *ye* believe," said the Lord, " which receive honour *one of another*, and not the honour that cometh from *God only* " (John v. 44) ?

Far be it from thee to have it said of thee, " Verily, thou hast thy reward " (Matt. vi. 5). May it rather be in your heart to say, with the Lord, " If I honour myself, my honour is nothing" (John viii. 54).

The man who is puffed up by empty praise is himself empty ; full of nothing but the wind of pride. If, therefore, you have anything of which you may justly be proud, glory not in thyself, but in the Lord from Whom

---

* That is, to the Divine Source of their strength and authority. Ed.

thou hast received it (1 Cor. i. 31); and say within thy-self, and with St. Paul, "By the grace of God I am what I am" (1 Cor. xv. 10). However many thy gifts may be, beware of being puffed up by them, and re-member the saying of the Lord, "I beheld Satan as lightning fall from Heaven" (Luke x. 18). "If I must needs glory," says the Apostle, "I will glory in my infirmities" (2 Cor. xi. 30). For it is the glory of the prelate to esteem himself miserable and weak; unequal to his burden *(onus)*, and unworthy of the honour *(honor)* thereof.

2. It is a common cause of pride (Origen in Ezek. hom. 9) for one who is ignorant to become the receiver of ecclesiastical dignities. How many there are, who, having been made Presbyters, have lost all their humility; as though it were the object of their ordination that they might now cease to be humble! Whereas, on the contrary, they ought so much the *more* to have studied the grace of humility, on the very ground of their exaltation; as the Scripture saith, "The higher thou art, the *more* humble thyself" (Ecclus. iii. 20); and again, "If thou be made the master of a feast, lift not thyself up, but be among them as one of the rest" (Ecclus. xxxii. 1).

There are some men (Peter Blois—reference not given) who mistake honour for virtue, and ascribe to their own merits a place of eminence which it has been rather to the displeasure of God that they have attained. The assumption of honour has been a source of temp-tation to many, and the occasion of their ruin. Do thou, therefore, so preside over others that thou mayest profit them *(sic præsis ut prosis)*. Woe be to those who preside over others, unless God preside over *them !* Do thou resort oftentimes and in secret either to acts of discipline, or to tears, or to some other acts in which, apart from the eye of man, thou mayest engage thyself alone, and take upon thyself the burden of the Lord's service—for that were the basest of all *slaveries* to which you could engage yourself, in which all the licence of perfect *freedom* could be indulged in at will.

# CHAPTER VII.

*HOW GREATLY ALL REGARD FOR PRAISE IS TO BE DREADED.*

1. IT is notably the case that in everything (St. Chrysostom in Matt. hom. 43. Apoc.) there springs forth from the midst of it that which is its ruin; as for example in the case of wood, there grows up from the bosom of the wood itself the grub which devours it. From the fabric of one's clothing comes forth the moth which eats the cloth; and from the garden-stuff comes forth the caterpillar which eats the garden-stuff. And it is the same in things spiritual. From the very purpose of our soul itself the enemy takes occasion to weave a net for our ruin; seeing that of himself he can do nothing, except we provide him with the occasion. Consequently he makes his approach to each man separately, according to his condition and state of life. Thus, for example, among warriors, out of their natural valour there comes forth strife and contention; among men of rank, from their desire for honour there springs forth envy; among the rich, out of their covetousness comes forth jealousy. In like manner in the case of Priests, who are set for the benefit of the people and for an instrument of their

sanctification, they are by their very office subject to the assaults of the Devil, so that what was designed for the edification of the people turns to their harm. Take away, then, this vice from the Clergy, that they should concern themselves to please the people, and they will have the less difficulty in contending with their faults.

2. The faithful High Priest (St. Bernard de mor. et offic. Episc. c. 3 ; compare also Greg. de cur. past. ii. 8) regarding with an eye of affection the gifts and blessings which pass through his hands to others, whether in the shape of divine blessings to men, or of offerings of men to God, still retains nothing of them whatever for himself. He seeks not the gifts of the people, but their profit ; and usurps not to himself the glory that is due to God (Phil. iv. 17). He does not " lay up his talent in a napkin " (Luke xix. 20), but " puts his money to the exchangers," that at his Lord's coming He may receive His own with usury (Matt. xxv. 27). He has no " holes " such as the foxes have, nor a " nest " as the birds ; no " bag," as Judas, nor " room in the inn," such as there was *not* for Mary. He resembles Him Who had not where to lay His Head (Matt. viii. 20) ; seeming for the present as a " despised and broken vessel," but destined in the future to be a vessel of honour. In a word, he parts, as it were, with his life in this present world, that he may preserve it in the world to come. No man can justly boast of this excellent gift of inward purity, until he has first wholly despised the vain glories of the outward man ; for he cannot truly devote himself to the service of God and

of his fellow man, until he has put aside all regard for his own. He alone can escape being defrauded of the glory of his inner purity of soul, who can say with the Lord, "If I seek my own glory, my glory is nothing" (John viii. 54), and with the Apostle, "To me to live is Christ, and to die is gain" (Phil. i. 21).

# CHAPTER VIII.

### ON SUNDRY OTHER SPECIAL REASONS WHICH EXIST FOR THE GRACES OF HUMILITY, AND THE FEAR OF GOD.

1. HOWEVER irreprehensible our undertaking of the clerical office may have been in the first instance, and however pure our intentions in so doing (St. Bernard Colloq. Simonis cum Jesu c. 16. Apoc.), is there, I would ask, nothing more to be afraid of? I answer, *much* indeed, and to be *feared* much. For not only is it not the case that every one who begins with the Spirit is therefore made perfect in the Spirit, but it is not unfrequently the case that he comes to be made perfect in the flesh (Gal. iii. 3). Saul, for example, was made a king by the Lord Himself (1 Kings xix. 17), and Judas, chosen by no other hand, is recorded to have been made an apostle. " Have I not chosen you twelve," our Lord said, " and one of you is a devil ? " (John vi. 71). O that one in twelve in our own day might be found a Peter, who should " forsake all things " (Matt. iv. 20), one who should have no " bag," as Judas, that he should " bear that which is put therein " (John xii. 46).

2. Consider then, what thou art, and of what thou

art made (St. Bernard de consid. ii. 5). As to the latter, indeed, I may esteem it the less worthy of notice, and leave it therefore to your own consideration. The consideration of what you *are* will lead you to a contempt for honour, even when in the very midst of it. And this is a great point. Let it not escape you. It is your shield against that very arrow itself. " Man being in honour hath no understanding" (Ps. xlix. 20). Say therefore to thyself: " I was an outcast in the House of my God " (Ps. lxxxiv. 10).* For what is your position but to be elevated from a condition of poverty and contempt " to be set over nations and kingdoms " (Jer. i. 10). And again, " Who am I, or what is my Father's house, that I should be set up on high over the people " (1 Kings ix. 21) ? It is evident, too, that He Who hath said unto me, " *Friend*, go up higher " (Luke xiv. 10), relied upon my being His friend. If I am found deficient in this respect, it is not expedient for me to glory. He " Who has set me up, can," if He will, " cast me down " (Ps. ci. 10). It is idle to flatter myself on an elevation which only increases my cares. The elevation itself is a peril to the soul : the cares attending it are the trials of its strength. Let us be girt around then with this grace, if we would not be sent down into "the lowest room."†

---

\* Latin " Abjectus eram in Domo Dei mei." Vulg.

† The translator has retained this short chapter, although only a continuation of previous thoughts, on the ground of its useful illustration of the patristic treatment of Holy Scripture.

# CHAPTER IX.

---

## THAT THE PRIEST SHOULD BE SOBER, AND AVOID FESTIVITY.

---

1. IF I find a Priest (St. Greg. Nyssen, de vitâ Moysis, pars ult :) redolent with ointments, adorned with rich apparel (silk) and indulging in costly feasts, I am justified in not detecting in him (to adopt the figure of the Evangelist) the true sacerdotal *tree* (cf. Matt. vii. 17) ; for such assuredly is not the *fruit* which the genuine tree of the Priesthood bears.

Is it not an anomaly and a disgrace to preach the poor and hungering Master Jesus Christ (St. Jerome in Micah ii. 9), and the doctrine of fasting and self-denial, with a distended belly and a bloated face, after the fashion of the world ?  If we stand in the place of the Apostles, let us imitate, not their discourse merely, but their conversation and manner of life also, and adopt their abstinence and sobriety.

Born, though I was, might the Lord say, in an humble cottage (St. Jerome, Ep. 34 ad Nepot, No. 6) and in a rural village, and scarcely able to satisfy nature, I now revel (in the person of My priest) in honey and fine flour.

2. Feasts given for love's sake are duly praised by all (St. Greg. Mag. Ep. lii. 2. 10 ad Greg. Natal, Episc. Salonicæ). Nevertheless it is necessary to observe that such is only just praise, when the lives of absent persons are not bitten by slanders, where no one is laughed at, and no silly stories are told about worldly matters, but the time is spent in listening to religious readings; where the body is not indulged more than is necessary, but its infirmities simply supplied, so as to qualify it for the practice of virtuous deeds. This if you observe in your convivial meetings, I freely acknowledge you are masters in abstinence.

Job knew (St. Greg. Mag. Moral. in Job iv. 3) that while festive occasions can rarely take place without some blame, there would consequently be much need of subsequent cleansing by means of sacrifices (Job. i. 5). For there are some faults which can scarcely be escaped by the members of a festive gathering, or even be avoided at all; seeing that some degree of pleasure is almost always associated with feasting; and when the body is relaxed by the delight which accompanies its refreshment, the heart is apt to give way to a frivolous joy. Hence it is written, " The people sat down to eat and drink, and rose up to play " (Exod. xxxii. 6). Light conversation, too, almost invariably accompanies feasting, and when the belly is satisfied, then the tongue is apt to be unbridled.

A chapter implying compulsory celibacy is here omitted, mainly from St. Bernard, as although calculated to recommend single life, where there seems a call to it, yet is alien from the conditions of our own Church. Whatever is retained, as *in the chapter following*, is equally applicable to the married as to the single life, and to clergy free to adopt either at their discretion. Ed.

# CHAPTER X.

1. NE of the chief trials of the Clergy in the matter of purity of life (Jerome ad Oceanum de vitâ Clericorum. Apoc.) arises from an allowance of the *too frequent* access of women; for it is impossible for the Priest who has undertaken the charge of the entire flock (Matt. xvi. 15), to occupy his time with the men only, and to *neglect* the women. On the contrary it is necessary, with the view to their salvation, that he should devote as much time to them, if not more, in the care of their souls. He must visit them in sickness, comfort them in sorrow, arouse them in neglectfulness; and, in the performance of all these duties, the evil spirit may find many opportunities of access to his soul, if he have not fortified it with the utmost and most exact care; for the eye of a woman is apt to influence and to disturb the mind, even though she be of ever so modest a character. But I do not say this (St. Basil, reg. brev. 109) because I forebode evil in thee, or in any other holy person; but simply because both good and evil are to be found in every condition and in every grade and sex; and to condemn the evil is, in effect, to praise the good.

2. So walk, then, and so conduct yourselves, that the Clerical office may suffer no stain from your manner of life! Let a *special* strictness as regards the company of women characterize your lives. Let authority direct your course, firmness be maintained in it, and gravity win for you a due respect. And, finally, " Whatsoever things are true, whatsoever things are honest, whatsoever things are just, whatsoever things are pure, whatsoever things are lovely, whatsoever things are of good report'; if there be any virtue, if there be any praise, think on these things " (Phil. iv. 8).

# CHAPTER XI.

## ON THE NECESSITY AND OBLIGATION OF UNFEIGNED CHARITY.

I. **W**HILST, then, the conspicuous beauty of holy chastity (St. Bernard de mor : et off : Episc. iii. 9) shines forth in your life and conduct, remember that without charity it has neither value nor merit. Neither indeed is this to be wondered at ; for what is there of good in anything that we undertake, if this grace be wanting? Is there any in faith ? "Though I had faith, so that I could remove mountains," there would be nothing (1 Cor. xiii. 2). Is there any in mere knowledge ? Not "though I should speak with the tongues of Angels" (ibid v. 1). In martyrdom? "Not," says the same Apostle, "though I should give my body to be burned" (ib. v. 3). Neither without it can anything that is really good be taken in hand, while, with it, the smallest matter may not be despised. Even chastity, without charity, is as a lamp without any oil (Matt. xxv. 3). Remove the oil and the lamp goes out : remove charity, and chastity itself at once ceases to please. But, on the other hand, " How beautiful," says the wise man, " is a chaste generation with charity" (Wisdom iv. 1)! " With

charity," I say, such as the Apostle describes as coming
"out of a *pure* heart, and of a good conscience, and of
faith unfeigned " (1 Tim. i. 5).

2. It further becomes the Priest to be hospitable
(St. Ambr. de off. min. lib. ii. 21, 106), kind, and just
(Tit. i. 8) ; not desirous of other men's goods (1 Tim.
iii. 3) ; nay, surrendering somewhat of his own rights,
where any dispute arises, rather than touching anyone
else's ;—avoiding litigation, abhorring disputes, and
purchasing concord and tranquillity at any price.  Indeed to surrender one's own rights is more often an
advantage to one's self, quite as much as it is a sacrifice.  For, in the first place, to put an end to the
mere cost of litigation is often a greater gain than to
succeed in it.  But besides that, it results in amity,
instead of in alienation,—a circumstance attended with
many and great advantages, which one who disregards
mere temporal ones will be glad to enjoy at any cost.

3. Beware (St. Jerome, Ep. 34 ad Nep. 14) of an
itching tongue, as well as of itching ears (2 Tim. iv. 3) ;
that is to say, neither injure any man's reputation, nor
listen to such injury from others.  " Thou satest and
spakest against thy brother, yea, and hast slandered
thine own mother's son.  These things hast thou done,
and I held my tongue, and thou thoughtest wickedly
that I am even such an one as thyself; but I will reprove
thee, and set before thee the things that thou hast done "
(Ps. l. 20, 21).  " Withhold thy tongue from detraction "
(Wisd. i. 11) ; and "keep thy mouth with all diligence "
(Prov. vii. 1) ;  and know that by whatsoever thou speak-

est against others, thou shalt thyself be judged, and shalt
be reproved in those selfsame matters wherein thou hast
contended with thy brother (cf. Rom. ii. 1).

Neither canst thou justly excuse thyself by saying that
thou canst not be doing an injury to a man by listening
to scandals that proceed from the lips of others.    No
one is very ready to tell stories to an unwilling hearer.
An arrow cannot be shot into a stone.    Nay, not unfrequently, it may rebound from it to the injury of the man
who shot it.    Let the detractor learn, when he sees thee
to be an unwilling hearer, *to be more sparing of his detraction!*    "With detractors," says Solomon, "be not
thou mixed up; for their calamity shall come suddenly,
and who knoweth the ruin of them both" (Prov. xxiv.
21, 22. Vulg.) ?    A question this, that may be asked as
much of him that willingly heareth, as of him that
uttereth a scandal.

E

# CHAPTER XII.

*ON THE DUTY OF OBEYING OUR SUPERIORS.*

I. **I**T is both difficult and altogether uncommon (St. Bern. de mor. et off. Episc. c. 8 and 9 No. 30 et sqq.) for one who is in a high position to do otherwise than think highly of himself. But the more rare his excellence is, so much the more noble is it. Accordingly let a modest fear of being unequal to the high position already attained by you, cause you to dread rather than to be pleased with the thought of a higher one. Do not therefore so much reckon yourselves to be happy in the possession of your present lofty position *(quia praestis)*, as unhappy if you do not turn it to good account *(prodestis)*. That you may, however, occupy that position with the more safety to yourselves, do not disdain to be subject to others, if there be any who have a claim to that submission from you ; for a dislike of subjection makes a man unworthy of any elevated position whatever. It is the counsel of the wise man, " The higher thou art, *the more humble thyself*" (Eccles. iii. 20), and it is the precept of Wisdom Itself, " Let him that is greatest among you, be as he that is least " (Luke xxii. 26). If therefore it be expedient to be subject to one's inferiors,

how can it be right to refuse the yoke of our superiors?
Rather let those who are subject to *you*, see in your *own*
conduct what their subjection to you should be. Understand ye what I say? " Honour to whom honour is
due " (Rom. xiii. 7). " Let every soul be subject unto
the higher powers " (Rom. xiii. 1): If *every* soul, then,
of course, *yours*. Who has exempted *you* from the rule
of all men? If any one attempts to make himself an
exception, he attempts to *defraud*. Consent not ye to
the counsels of those, who, while calling themselves
Christians, nevertheless account it a disgrace either to
imitate the example of Christ or to obey His word.

2. " Render," He says, " unto Cæsar the things that
are Cæsar's, and unto God the things that are God's "
(Matt. xxii. 21). And what He thus uttered with His
lips, He presently carried out with the same lips that
uttered it. The Creator of Cæsar hesitated not to pay
tribute *to* Cæsar; and in so doing He gave us an example
that we should do as He had done (Matt. xvii. 26, and
John xiii. 15). When, too, did He ever refuse the
reverence due to the Priests of God, Who was so
careful not to refuse it to the secular power? Moreover, it would be unbecoming in you, who submit yourselves to the successor of Cæsar, that is, to the reigning
King, being active in his courts, in his counsels, in his
affairs, and in his armies, to show yourselves to any
representative *(Vicario)* of Christ otherwise than has
been ordained from all antiquity in His Churches.

3. How beautifully did the blessed Centurion express
himself, to whose faith no equal was found in Israel!

" I also," he said, "am a man under authority, having
soldiers under me " (Matt. viii. 9).  He made no boast
of his own power, which he did not mention alone, nor
even first ; for intending to say presently that he had
" soldiers under him," he first spoke of himself as being
a man " *under authority*."   He first spoke of himself as
a *man*, and then as one under the authority of *others*.
This Gentile, I observe, first called himself a man, that
he might show that in his person that was fulfilled which
David had said long before: " Let the heathen know
themselves to be but men " (Ps. ix. 20) !   " I am a *man*,"
he said, and a man, too, " *under authority*."   Already
then, you will have perceived, we have not convicted
him of boasting in this matter.   Humility has been
foremost in his case, lest, being exalted, he should have
been cast down.   And in truth no place was found in
him for arrogance, where humility had found so conspicuous a seat.

# CHAPTER XIII.

*ON THE NEED WHICH A PRIEST HAS OF A WISE
DIRECTOR AND GOOD ADVISERS.*

I. YOU will have done wisely (St. Bern. de mor.
et off. Episc. i. 3) if you have concluded
that the office of a Priest, and the pastoral
care attaching thereto, cannot be well undertaken without good advice (cf. Ecclus. xxxii. 24). Hence it is that
Wisdom herself, the Parent of wise counsels, speaking
of herself, says : " I Wisdom dwell with prudence and
find out the knowledge of witty inventions " (Prov.
viii. 12); for such is the knowledge and wisdom in
which she is exercised. But that infidel counsels are
to be shunned by her she advises us by the mouth of
Solomon, where he says : " Debate thy cause with thy
neighbour himself, and discover not a secret to another "
(Prov. xxv. 9). And well, too, does she say by the
mouth of another sage, when counselling her hearers
to do nothing without advice, yet at the same time
intimating the scarcity of such advisers,—" Have many
friends, but let thy *counsellor* be one among a thousand "
(Eccles. vi. 6). *"One,"* you observe, "among a *thousand.*"

Let it be, therefore, with you a matter of the utmost
concern (St. Basil, de abdic : rerum) that you seek out

some man whom you may follow as an adviser in all the pursuits of the life which you have chosen ; and one who can safely point out the true pathway to God, to all such as desire truly to walk therein :—one who shall be adorned with virtues, and whose whole manner of life shall bear witness to the love of God which dwells within him :—one, moreover, who is well versed in all holy learning, whose mind is not puffed up with vainglory, nor influenced by flattery, but is ever strict and consistent ; and one, lastly, who sets the glory of God before all else.    If by the blessing of God you have found such a counsellor as this—and, doubtless, if it is your *desire* to do so, you *will*—and a master (as he should be) in good works, keep him constantly by you, and neglect not his advice.

2.    There are those who trust no one but themselves (which is the worst thing they can do), and only account *that* advice to be good which comes of their *own mind*. It is the saying of Wisdom :—" The way of a fool is right in his own eyes ; " " but the Lord searcheth the hearts " (Prov. xiii. 15 and xxi. 2).    And again :—" There is a way which seemeth right unto a man, but the end thereof are the ways of death " (Prov. xvi. 25). Let us beware (St. Aug. de doct. Christ. Prologue 6) of such haughty and perilous temptations, and prefer rather the case of St. Paul, who, although cast to the ground and instructed by the Divine and Heavenly Voice, was nevertheless sent for instruction to a man (Acts ix. 17).

Think, again, of the Centurion Cornelius, whose

prayers were heard, and whose alms were reported by the Angel; yet he was sent to Peter to be instructed (Acts x. 4 and 5). Did not Moses in like manner converse with God? Yet he modestly received counsel from his father-in-law in the matter of the ruling and administration of that vast multitude, although one of another race than his own (Exod. xviii. 18). Let all things, then, be done by you with counsel and modest consideration, and in all cases be guided, not by your own spirit, but by the Spirit of God, by which "the sons of God are led" (Rom. viii. 14).

# CHAPTER XIV.

*ON THE CHARACTER OF HIS INTIMATES, WHOM TO AVOID, AND WHOM TO CHOOSE.*

1. ACCORDING to the precept of our Lord (St. Bern. de mor: et off: Episc. i. 2), we are to love our enemies, but are only to accept for our advisers such as appear prudent and men of good will. On this account the Lord refuted the imprudent counsel of His disciple, and the unbelieving counsel of His brethren, saying to the one, " Thou savourest not of the things that be of God " (Matt. xvi. 23) ; and to the unbelieving, " Go ye up unto this feast : I go not up yet unto this feast " (John vii. 8). He trusted not Himself either to the malice of the one, or to the imprudence of the other. Seeking, in short, to whom He should entrust Himself, and to whom He could safely confide the dispensation of His Mysteries, and seeming to find it a difficult matter, He asks, as it were, in astonishment, " *Who* is that faithful and wise servant, whom his Lord shall set over His household " (Matt. xxi. 45) ? Wherefore, also, on entrusting His Sheep to the care of Peter, He took care first of all to make proof of his good-will by asking him three times if he loved Him (John xxi. 16). He tested

his prudence, too, in like manner, when, on men's committing mistakes and fancying Him to be one of the prophets risen from the dead, He asked them, saying : " But whom say *ye* that I am ? " To Whom Peter answered, declaring Him plainly to be the God of the Prophets, and saying, " Thou art the Christ, the Son of God " (Matt. xvi. 16).

2. There are some, indeed (St. Aug. Ep. 208 ad Felic. 2), who occupy the pastoral chair for the sole benefit of the flock of Christ; but others there are, who do so only for their own personal profit. It cannot but be that these two classes of pastors will continue to minister from time to time in the Church of Christ even to the end, and to the day of judgment itself. For, if there were such in the days of the Apostles, over whom the Apostle Paul groaned, and spoke of them to the Corinthians (2 Cor. xi. 26) as " false brethren," yet all the while never haughtily separated himself from them, but tolerated and endured them; how much more reason is there that we should find it the same in our own times, seeing that the Lord hath plainly said, with reference to these times, that " Because iniquity shall abound, the love of many shall wax cold " (Matt. xxiv. 12). But what follows is both a comfort and a warning to us :—" He that persevereth unto the end, the same shall be saved " (Matt. xxiv. 13).

Let poor travellers and the like, and, with them, as it will assuredly be, Christ Himself, be present at your table, and be partakers of your plain fare. Shun, as a plague, a Clerical usurer—a man that grows rich (on his office) from a state of poverty, and has become conspicuous from a mean condition. " Evil communications corrupt good manners" (1 Cor. xv. 33). You despise money : the other loves it. You spurn wealth : the other runs after it. You are a lover of silence, of gentleness, of privacy : he of verbosity, and of the impudent face, the markets, the fairs, and the public resorts. What agreement can there possibly be, where there is such a diversity of habit ? Let us hold fast then, to the companionship (St. Ambr. de off. min. i. 43. No. 221) of the most praiseworthy of our elders in the ministry ! For while the society of our equals is the more agreeable to us, that of our elders is in proportion the more safe :—men, who by a certain position of superiority and by their general manner of life give a colour to the habits of their younger brethren, and, as it were, impart to them a dye of virtuous conduct. For if those who are as yet in need of guidance in roads unknown to them, prefer the companionship and guidance of others, who are better acquainted with them, how much more should young men seek to walk in new roads in the company of their seniors, that they may be the less likely to wander astray and go wrong in the path of virtue ! There is nothing more delightful than to have such men as these, both as guides and as examples to us in their daily life.

# CHAPTER XV.

*THAT A PRIEST OUGHT TO BE MODEST.*

1. IT is desirable (St. Ambr. de off. Min. lib. 1. cap. ult. 255) that the public at large should be witnesses of our manner of life, so that nothing should be said abroad to the scandal of our office, and that the man who observes the Minister of the Altar to be adorned with becoming virtues, should be led to reverence the Lord Himself, Who has such men for His servants. For it is to the praise of God when His house is unsullied by scandals and the discipline of His family is unblameable.

2. In a prominent place, too, amongst our efforts (St. Basil. Ep. i. ad St. Greg. Naz : de vitâ solit.) it should be our endeavour so to regulate our conversation as not to indulge in long controversies, nor in sharp answers, nor in upbraiding our adversary, nor in interrupting his words for the purpose of a hasty and vain display of one's self. We ought to learn, without being ashamed of it, whatever we do not know, and to teach with all charity whatever we do know, without pretending to be ignorant of it. If some severity be occasionally needed, yet let there be no bitterness.

3. Neither do I persuade you to use austerity (St.

Bern. De consid. ii. No. 22), but rather gravity. The
former repels the weak; the latter puts a check on such
as are disposed to trifle. The former, if it be resorted
to, makes one disliked; the latter, if it be wanting, contemptible. In all things let there be moderation. I
would neither be too severe nor too lenient. What is
more pleasing than this happy mediocrity, so as neither
to become burdensome by over-much severity, nor contemptible by familiarity. To put a guard on one's
mouth is always useful (Ecclus. xxii. 23), but this does
not forbid us the grace of affability. On all occasions,
however, to put a curb on one's tongue is our first duty,
especially at any convivial gathering. Such is your
most suitable and becoming habit, if at least you be
strict in action, calm in countenance, and serious in
your words.

4. If our minds and spirits must be pleased (St.
Aug de Symb. ad catech. (Apocr.) i. c. 2, 3) our Holy
Mother the Church sets before us worthy *(veneranda)*
and wholesome objects; such as shall afford our minds
sufficient pleasure and tend rather to preserve than to
corrupt our faith. I have read, says St. Jerome (on
the Prophet Micah v. 7, and on Ps. xc.) that the fisher-
man is holy, but not the hunter. It is clear, indeed,
that another sort of hunting devolves upon you as a
duty of your calling, in the success of which stands the
salvation of its objects, and the credit of their pursuer.
For what saith the Lord by His Prophet? " Behold,
I send forth *hunters*, and they shall hunt you upon every
mountain " (Jeremiah xvi. 16). And of a truth the

Prelates of the Church do so "hunt upon every mountain," when they catch hold on wandering souls, like prey, to the obedience of Christ, from the "high places" of science and worldly learning. The Apostles, sent forth into the whole world (Mark xvi. 15), pursued with their preaching the wild beasts of the marshes, when, after the example of their Master, they reproved the hypocrisy of the Pharisees, and, chiding them for their empty outward observance of a merely figurative ceremonial, gathered by their hunting in one day many thousands of men to the faith of Christ.

O that you may in likewise manner devote yourselves with a good will to this sort of hunting, and make up, it may be, for the loss of a long period of time, which has been wasted in vanity, by the results of a better life and the building up of the people.

END OF BOOK I.

# Book II.

# On the Pastoral Care.

## CHAPTER I.

*THAT THE PASTORAL CHARGE IS ONE OF PERIL,
AS SHOWN BY THE EXAMPLE OF THE SAINTS
AND BY THE TEACHING OF CHRIST.*

1. BEFORE all things I demand (St. Aug. Ep. 21 ad Valer. No. 4) that your devout prudence will bear in mind that there is nothing in this life, and especially in these times, more easy and pleasant or more acceptable to mankind in general than the office of a Bishop, Priest, or Deacon, provided only that it be discharged in a perfunctory and inoffensive manner. But then, it must be borne in mind, on the other hand, that there is nothing more hateful than this state of things in the sight of God, or more lamentable and disreputable in itself. I would have you beware, too, that there is nothing in this life, and especially in these days, more difficult and laborious, or more fraught with peril than these sacred offices; but at the same time, nothing, more blessed of God, provided they be bravely carried out *(militentur)* in that

F

particular manner which our Commander-in-chief has prescribed to us.

2. There is no one (St. Chrys. de Sac. iii. 7) who ever loved Christ more vehemently than the Apostle Paul, and no one who was more acceptable than he in the sight of God; nevertheless, after receiving such privileges as he did at the Hands of God, he trembled, and was grievously afraid of the lofty position in which he was thus placed, for the sake of those who were subjected to him. "I fear," he said, "lest it should come to pass that, as the Serpent deceived Eve by his subtlety, so your minds should be corrupted from the simplicity which is in Christ" (2 Cor. xi. 3).

Such are the words that this man uttered, to whom nevertheless it had been granted by God that he should be snatched up into the third Heaven, and be made a partaker of divine Secrets (2 Cor. xii. 4); who endured, as I may say, as many deaths as he lived days after his first believing in Christ (1 Cor. xv. 31); who also himself shrank from making use of the power given to him by God Himself, lest he should offend any of those persons who had pledged their faith to Christ (1 Cor. ix. 12).

If, then, Paul, while keeping in this scrupulous way the strict injunctions of God, even to the extent of adding others besides to them, and never in any degree consulting his own interests, but those of his hearers only, was thus in a constant state of trepidation, what shall such as we do, who are engaged, so many of us, in studying our own interests, and not only fail to keep entire the commandments of Christ, after His noble example, but even largely transgress them? "Who is weak," says the Apostle, "and I am not weak? Who is offended and I burn not?" (2 Cor. xi. 2). Such manifestly should be the character and disposition of every priest.

3. To a king men's bodies are entrusted, to a Priest their souls. A king may spare his subjects the wounds of bodily chastisement, but a Priest heals the wounds of the soul. The one compels by force; the other constrains by exhortation; the one by authority, the other by advice. The one carries bodily armour, the other spiritual. The one wages war with barbarians, the other with demons. This latter, then, of a surety is the higher function. Hence it is that the king places his head in the hands of the Priest (at his coronation), and it is everywhere recorded in Holy Scripture that the Priests anointed the kings.

4. It was by no means without purpose that those words of our Lord were so often repeated (St. Chrys. in Is. hom. iv. No. 5), "Peter, *lovest* thou Me," when the Lord committed unto him His Sheep (John xxi. 15). And I understand Him to have meant by these words, that except on the testimony of his conscience he *did* so love Him perfectly and supremely, that is to say, more devotedly than all his temporal possessions, and more than all his relatives and friends—nay, more than his very own self—(that I may thus fill up the measure of His meaning), he should on no account undertake this sacred charge, nor meddle with the sheep for whom His very Blood was to be shed.

Terrible words, surely, are these, and enough to make the hearts of the very boldest tyrants tremble with fear?

Wherefore, I beseech you, take heed to yourselves, whosoever you be to whom this sacred ministry has been committed;—take heed, I say, to yourselves, and to the charge which has been laid upon you! It is a city that you have the care of (Cant. iii. 3, Is. lxii. 12, Matt. v. 14 and xii. 25); watch ye therefore over its safety and over its unanimity! It is a Bride (Cant. iv. 8, Rev. xxii. 9). Study ye therefore her adornment! It is a flock of sheep (John xxi. 17). Have a care therefore of their pasture. And these three warnings of mine will not probably be judged out of character with the three-fold question of our Lord, as put to His Apostle.

5. St. John in his Epistle (St. Aug. on St. John, Tract. xlvii. 2) has said:—" As Christ laid down His Life for us, so we also ought to lay down our lives for the brethren" (1 John iii. 16). Hence in a certain place it is written:—" When thou sittest down to meat at a great man's table, consider diligently what is before thee; and put thine hand to thy mouth, if thou be a man given to appetite" (Prov. xxiii. 1). You all know what is the Table of the Almighty. Is it not that of the Body and Blood of Christ? Let the man, then, who sitteth at such a Table as that, make due preparation! But what meaneth this? It meaneth that, as He laid down His own life for us, so should we also be *ready* to lay down our lives for the edification of the people, and for the defence of the faith. Hence when

He would appoint Peter to be a good shepherd, what saith He? " Peter, *lovest* thou Me? Feed My sheep" (John xxi. 17). Once, twice, three times, did He say these words, till Peter was grieved at His saying them. And when the Lord had thus questioned him as far as He judged sufficient, that his three-fold confession might correspond to his previous three-fold denial, and He had thus thrice committed His sheep to his charge, at last He said to him :—" When thou wast young, thou girdest thyself, and walkedst whither thou wouldest, but when thou shalt be old, thou shalt stretch forth thine hands and another shall gird thee, and carry thee whither thou wouldest not." And the Evangelist then explains these words of the Lord thus:—" This He said, signifying by what death he should glorify God " (John xx. 18, 19). Agreeably to this explanation, the word " Feed My sheep " would seem to mean, in effect, that he should lay down his life for them.

# CHAPTER II.

*THAT PASTORS HAVE TO UNDERGO A STRICT EXAM-
INATION AND TO RENDER AN EXACT ACCOUNT
OF THEIR CONDUCT, AFTER DEATH.*

1. GREAT is the dignity of the Priests (St.
Jerome, comment: in Ezekiel xliv.), but
great is their fall, if they err. We may
well congratulate ourselves on our elevation, but fear
and tremble at a fall. It is not a matter of so great
rejoicing, that of our having attained our elevation, as
it is of sorrow and dismay in the case of our fall. For
not only shall we have to render an account of our own
faults (Luke xvi. 2), but of the faults of all those on
whose gifts we live, but for whose salvation we have
not cared.

What more delightful than Paradise! What safer
than Heaven! Yet a man fell from Paradise, and an
Angel from Heaven, only through sinning! " Great
men shall be greatly tormented," saith Solomon (Wisdom vi. 7). More is required from a Priest than from
a Deacon (Origen, hom. xi. on Jerem.), more from a
Deacon than from a layman; but the Ecclesiastic who
attains to the highest dignity in the whole Church, will
have to render an account of the whole.

If (St. Chrys. hom. iii. in Act. Apost. No. 5) thou sinnest as a private person, thou wilt not suffer these things; but, if in the Priesthood, thou hast perished. Consider how many things Moses endured, in how many things he proved himself superior to the magicians, and how eminent he was in good works; yet, only because he committed one sin, he was severely punished (Numb. xx. 12); and that with reason, because it was to the injury of others. He suffered the more severe penalty, not merely on account of the sin being openly committed, but because it was the sin of a Priest.

2. I tell you, my brethren (St. Bern. Serm. in Conc. Rhem. No. 1. Apocr.), God has highly exalted you. "Ye are the salt of the earth," as saith the Lord. "Ye are the light of the world" (Matt. v. 13, 14). "I have said, Ye are gods, and ye are all the children of the Most High; but ye shall die like men, and ye shall fall like one of the princes" (Ps. lxxxii. 6, 7). "Where is the wise? Where is the scribe? Where is the disputer of this world" (1 Cor. i. 20)? Shall they not indeed all die like men? And shall they not fall like one of the princes? But whence shall they fall, and whither? Will it not be from the Right Hand of God, and into the depths of Hell?

My brethren, there remains to us all two evils—death and the judgment. For hard indeed is the condition of death, so that it rarely happens that a man wishes to die. But what remedy is there for death, seeing that it is the way of all flesh? "Whither shall I go from

Thy Spirit? or whither shall I flee from Thy Presence"
(Psalm cxxxviii. 7)? Doth not the Apostle say:—"We
must all stand before the judgment seat of Christ, that
every man may give an account of his own works done
in the body, whether they be good or evil" (2 Cor. v.
20)? My brethren, I am speaking to you of the great
gathering together of all men, when the Lord God
shall sit in judgment, and when we must all stand
before Him, and "God shall judge the world in righteousness" in that final assize, and we must *all* of us
stand there, everyone in his own person, whether he be
Pope, or Cardinal, or Archbishop, or Bishop, Priest, or
Deacon; whether he be rich or poor, learned or unlearned, that every man may give account of his *own
deeds* done in the body, whether they be good or evil. And,
if this be so, alas! what will become of those deeds
which they have done, not merely in their own bodies,
but in the Body of Christ, which is His Church?

3. The glory of this world passeth away; all its
ambition passeth away (St. Aug. Ep. 23 ad Max.).
In the future judgment of Christ, lofty thrones and
gorgeously-covered chairs will afford us no protection,
when once conscience has begun to accuse us, and
the Arbiter of consciences to pass judgment upon us.
Offices that men deemed honourable here will be treated
as responsibilities there. Matters which were recorded
to our honour here, as of utility to the Church, will be
justified, no doubt, by the testimony of a good conscience; but we shall be unable to defend what was
wrong.

You see with how severe a sword the world strikes at us (Greg. Mag. hom. 47 in Evangel.), and what heavy blows the people deal at us! But by whose fault? Whose, I say, if not ours? Look at the depopulated cities, the walls thrown down, the churches and monasteries destroyed, and the fields deserted! But we are the persons who are the authors of all this death and ruin to the perishing people, to whom we should have been as guides to eternal life. For is it not, indeed, through our fault that the multitude of the people is thus trodden down, because through our negligence they were not trained up in the ways of life? *

* These passages have been retained, although apparently irrelevant, as pointing distinctly and usefully, perhaps, to events of *our own former history*, as testified by our picturesque ruins and our overthrown monastic foundations. Ed.

# CHAPTER III.

*ON THE SAME SUBJECT.*

1. **B**UT (St. Greg. Mag. hom. xvii. in Evangel. in fine), however neglectful we may be, will Almighty God desert His own sheep? By no means, for He has promised to them by the mouth of His Prophet that He will feed them Himself (Ezek. xxxiv. 13); and everyone whom He hath "ordained to Eternal Life" (Acts xiii. 48) He will train up by those secret stirrings of compunction which He will for their good create within them. It is, however, through our instrumentality that the faithful come to receive Holy Baptism, that they are benefitted by our prayers, and through the imposition of our hands become receivers of the Holy Spirit and attain unto the kingdom of Heaven; but, behold! we ourselves through our negligence incline downwards! The elect advance forward under the blessing of the laying on of hands, while the Priests themselves, who thus minister to their salvation, fall into that ruin which is justly due to their own reprobate lives. To what, then, shall I say that these evil Priests are to be compared, but to the baptismal water, which, by washing away the sins of those who are baptized therein, admits them into the

kingdom of Heaven, but itself immediately after runs down into the sewers?

2. We who are esteemed to be somewhat (Origen in Jer. hom. 7. cf. Gal. ii. 2), that is, who preside over others in our clerical order (so much so that some persons of a lower rank in life are ambitious to be raised to the same with ourselves), ought however to know that we are not necessarily *saved* because we chance to be *ordained;* for there are many clergy who are lost, while many of the laity are found among the most highly blessed. Nevertheless, if we are duly qualified for the clerical office, let us also accept and undertake it. Seeing, however, that there are some clergy who do not so live as to derive any spiritual benefit from their ordination, or are any ornament whatever to their profession, there are some who interpret the Prophet Jeremiah (xii. 13) as saying concerning them: " Their clergy shall not profit them " (cf. lxx.). For the advantage of the clerical office does not consist in this, that they should be seated in the chair of the Presbytery, but that they should walk agreeably to their position and to the commandment of God.

Joshua commanded the children of Israel (Orig. hom. in Josh.) that they should keep at a distance of two thousand cubits from the Ark of the Covenant, but the Priests and Levites nearer ; and *so* near that the Ark of the Lord and the Book of the Covenant should be carried upon their shoulders (Josh. iii.). Happy are they who are accounted worthy to be set thus near to

God! But remember that it is written, "The Lord thy God is a consuming Fire" (Deut. iv. 24). If you were made of gold or silver, and you drew near to fire, you would shine all the more brilliantly for your nearness to it; but if, upon the foundation of the faith which is in you, you are conscious that you have built up nothing but wood, hay, and stubble, you would, on the approach of fire, only be consumed by it. Happy, then, are those Priests who are placed thus near to it, and it causes them to shine, but not to be burned.

3. We may well tremble at the description which the Prophet gives (St. Bernard, Serm. 23 in Cant. No. 42), where he speaks of God as addressing His angels, and saying, " Let favour be shown to the wicked, yet will he not learn righteousness. In the land of justice he will deal unjustly, and will not behold the glory of God " (Isaiah xxvi. 10).

Let then the clergy tremble! Let the ministers of the Church tremble, who in the very territory of the Saints which they occupy, so misbehave themselves, that, instead of being contented with their incomes, which ought to suffice them, they keep for their own use, impiously and sacrilegiously, what should be given to the poor, and are not afraid to spend upon their own luxuries what should supply the poor with bread;— sinning in this way with a two-fold iniquity, in that they thus rob others and spend that which is sacred on their own vanity and vice !

Seeing, then, that He " Whose judgments are a great

deep" (Ps. xxxvi. 6), bears long with such Priests as these, and is merciful to them only that He may not spare those in eternity who would thus seek repose here below, we are led rather to tremble than to feel secure at the contemplation of such cases.

ON THE DUTIES OF PASTORS TOWARDS GOD AND
TOWARDS MAN.

---

## CHAPTER I.

*ON ZEAL FOR THE SALVATION OF SOULS.*

1. IF (St. Jerome, Ep. 13 ad Paulin. No. 5) you desire to discharge the functions of the Priestly office, or should the office or the honours of the Episcopate chance to delight thee, let the salvation of other men's souls be the *one reward of thine own.* You should know (St. Athan. Ep. ad Dracont. Episc. fugientem), and by no means doubt it, that before you were ordained you lived only to yourself, but that since your ordination you live for those *for whose sake you were ordained.*

When the Lord (St. Cyril, Alex. on John iv. 32) said that it was His "meat to do the will of His Father, and to finish His work" (John iv. 34), which work was the salvation of men, He describes the character of the Apostolic Ministry. And because they were to be the masters of the world to come, He taught His Apostles after His own example, that they should care far more for the salvation of others' souls than for the welfare of their own bodies. Up to that time (St. Aug. contr.

Faust, xxxii. 10), it had been enjoined upon a man to marry his deceased brother's widow, that he might raise up seed, not to himself, but to his *brother*, and call them after his *brother's* name (Deut. xxv. 5 et seq.). By this law what else, I would ask, is signified to us, than that every preacher of the Gospel should so labour in the Church, that, now that his brother is dead, *i.e.*, Christ, he should raise up seed unto Him Who died for us (1 Thess. v. 10), which, when so raised up, should bear His Name? Christ has died. The Apostles (St. Aug. Serm. 380) have received His Bride the Church. Those whom they have begotten by her, are not called Paulians, or Petrians, after the names of those by whom they were begotten, but Christians. But the man who, when once chosen by the Church, declines from his duty of preaching the Gospel to the people, is rightly and religiously despised by the Church. For this is what is meant by the command that the widowed woman should spit in the face of her husband's brother; and—not without a signification of the like contempt to this—by the casting off of the shoe also; that by this action they may be separated from those of whom the Prophet speaks, saying: " How beautiful are the feet of them that preach the Gospel of Peace, that bring good tidings of good " (Is. lii. 7)! For the man who so retains the faith of the Gospel as to profit himself, and not refuse to profit the Church also, may be considered to be represented by the man who is shod on both his feet (cf. Eph. vi. 15). Whereas the man who considers that he has done all that is required, if he believes the Gospel for his own sake, while he refuses all concern for the salvation of others, is represented by the man who, to his reproach, has cast off one of his shoes.

2. My brethren (St. Greg. Mag. hom. 17 in Evang.), let our life be in accordance with our vocation. Let us seek daily the forgiveness of our faults. Let us consider unceasingly what we are, and devote ourselves to the study of our sacred office, and of the burden we have taken upon us. Let us consider daily the account we shall have to render to our Judge, and be only so careful of ourselves as not to neglect the care of our neighbour, that he may be benefitted by the salt of our conversation. When we meet with any one of a loose or lascivious character, he is to be warned that he should restrain his evil tendencies by marriage, so that by that which is lawful he may learn to conquer that which is unlawful. When we meet with one that is married, he is to be admonished that he only so devote himself to the concerns of this world as not to interfere with his love of God, only so far yield to the wishes of his wife, as not to displease God (1 Cor. vii. 33). When we meet with a Clergyman, he is to be exhorted to consider how far he is living so as to set a good example to the laity; lest, should there be anything reprehensible in his conduct and manner of life, our religion suffer thereby in public estimation. In short, no one should find himself in the presence of a Priest, *and leave it without some edification from his discourse.*

3. The soul of a righteous man (St. Bernard, Serm. in

Synod. No. 11. Apocr.) is the dwelling-place and Temple
of God (1 Cor. iii. 16 and John xiv. 23), and the Lord,
in this His Holy Temple, doeth wonders and delivereth
oracles. " Let the Lord," then, " Whom ye seek ; come
thus suddenly to His Temple" (Matt. iii. 1), that you
may be enabled by His Presence in you to resist the
temptations of the Devil. Let Him not fail therefore
to be admitted into this His Sanctuary by any of those
who are to Him as His very nearest relations—His
father, His mother, and His brethren ! But *who* are
these ? Let us hear His own words !—" Whosoever
doeth the will of My Father which is in Heaven ; the
same is My father, and mother, and brother, and sister "
(Matt. xii. 50) ;—His father, by the soul-begetting word
of preaching, as saith the Apostle, " I have begotten you
*in Christ ;* "—His mother, as bringing forth (souls) by the
example of a holy conversation ;—His brother and sister,
as loving Him and one another in brotherly affection (1
Pet. i. 22). Such relationships as these do ye bear to Him,
that are Priests in His Church; or such, at least, *ought* ye
to bear. The people have set you to be the mediators
between themselves and God, that He may thus speak
to you, and you to Him (Exod. xx. 19). For this purpose they give you their alms and first-fruits, that by
your prayers and the merit of your conversation He
may be propitiated towards them, and they may themselves be thus brought nearer to Him. If, then, you
are yourselves an offence to Him, how can you plead
effectually with Him for others ?

G

# CHAPTER II.

---

---

1. WHAT occupation, I would ask, can there possibly be of greater importance to mankind than the ministry of souls (St. Chrys. de Sac. ii. 1), which is represented to us by our Lord Himself as a sure testimony of love and devotion to His own Person? For, addressing the chief of the Apostles, He said, "Simon, son of Jonas, *lovest* thou Me?" And on his assenting thereto, He added: "If thou lovest Me, feed My sheep" (John xxi. 17). The master questions the disciple as to whether He is loved by him, not with the intention of ascertaining his disposition; for why should *He* desire to know *that*, "Who knoweth the very secrets of all hearts;" but that He might teach us how great a charge is that of the care of the souls of His flock. This assumed, it is easy to see how great are the rewards reserved for every one who shall have consecrated all his cares, all his labours, all his thoughts, and all the application of his soul to the work which Jesus Christ loves and esteems so highly.

2. Should any friend volunteer to undertake the care of our sheep of his own accord, could we question his affectionate devotion to our interests? Yet these sheep have cost us nothing but our money, while Jesus Christ has given for His, not money, or any similar exchange whatever, but *His own Life and His own Blood*. What reward, then, I would ask, may we believe that He will hereafter confer on the shepherds and guides of His flock, purchased, as it was, at so great a price? Hence, when Peter gave answer to the Lord, saying, " Thou *knowest*, Lord, that I love Thee," and thus appealed, as a sufficient testimony of his love, to the secret knowledge of the Lord Himself, the Saviour Jesus did not stop there, but claimed a still further testimony. Yet neither was it the object of the Divine Master merely to obtain proof as to how perfectly His Apostle loved Him, as is evident for various reasons; but His purpose was that by means of this conversation He should teach us all wherein consists the true manifestation of our love towards Him; namely, in the *charity and benevolence which we should display towards His Church, on the care of which we should bestow the whole devotion of our minds.*

3. For why was it that the Almighty and supremely good God should thus refuse to spare His Only Begotten Son the sufferings He endured (Rom. viii. 32)? Why, but that those who had incurred his displeasure by their wrong doings should be reconciled thereby to Himself, and become a chosen people in His sight (Tit. ii. 14)? For, for what purpose was it that He

shed His Blood? Was it not that He might gather
His flock to Himself, whom He then gave in charge to
Peter? Justly, therefore, and with good reason, did
Christ thus speak, saying :—" Who is that faithful and
wise servant whom his Lord shall set over His household" (Matt. xxiv. 45) ? But, again, these words seem
to have been uttered with some degree of hesitation,
although spoken by One Who was the least *given* to
hesitation. For, as He first demanded of Peter if he
loved Him, not merely to ascertain the trustworthiness
of Peter only, but to set before us all the true evidence
of our love towards Him in all times, so, when He here
puts the question, " Who is that faithful and wise
servant ? " He did not do so because He did not know
of His own knowledge the hearts of all men, but because
He wished thus to point out to all both how rare a
person such a servant was, and how great and how
extensive his charge.

4. Consider, then, how great a reward is in store for
the due exercise of this charge ! " He will set him,"
He saith, " over all that He hath." Do not contend
that this trust was not wisely or happily committed to
you, who are thus put in charge of all the flock and
property of the Lord ; especially so long as you act as
Peter did, whom, so long as he did so act, Christ
Himself clothed with authority, and gave him grace to
surpass all the rest of the Apostles ;—saying to him,
" Lovest thou Me more than these do ? " " Feed My
sheep." He might have said to him such words as
these :—" If thou lovest Me, give thyself to fasting ;

sleep upon the bare ground ; watch early and late ; be a father to the fatherless, and a husband to the widow." But, on the contrary, passing by all these secular duties, what saith He ?   " Feed My sheep ! "

# CHAPTER III.

-----

## AN EARNEST EXHORTATION TO PASTORS TO EXERCISE A TRUE PASTORAL CARE AND TÒ HAVE AN ANXIOUS THOUGHT FOR THEIR FLOCK.

-----

1. BUT, alas! I say it with sorrow (St. Greg. Mag. hom. xvii. in Evang.), what do we? We, who hasten for our salaries, but are idle at our work?—Who receive in our stipends the funds of the Church, but for the Everlasting Church itself labour but little in the matter of "the word and doctrine?" Let us consider what a crime it is to receive the rewards of labour, without labouring for them! Behold, we live on the offerings of the faithful, and shall we not labour for their souls? Is it not the case that we scarcely ever openly reprove any one for his or her sins, and sometimes, if one be in an exalted position and in power, we may chance even to smooth over, if not to praise his sins, lest, if we should estrange him from us, we should suffer personal loss?

2. Surely we have not forgotten (St. Greg. Mag. Ep. 49 ad Anast. Ep. Antioch. ix. 2) how the blessed Jacob, who served so long for his two wives, said, "I have been with thee these twenty years. Thy ewes and thy

she-goats have not cast their young: the rams of thy
flock I have not eaten : that which was torn of beasts,
I brought not unto thee : I bare the loss of it.  Of my
hand didst thou require it, whether stolen by day, or
stolen by night : I bore the heat of the day, and the
cold by night; and sleep departed from mine eyes "
(Gen. xxxi. 38, &c.).  Who among us, I would ask,
manifests a like solicitude for the sheep of Christ, as
Jacob did for those sheep of Laban ?

3. Let us, then, set before our mind's eye (St. Greg.
Mag. hom. xlvii. in Evang.) that day of solemn and
strict account, on which the Judge shall come, and
take an account of His servants to whom He had
entrusted His talents (Matt. xviii. 23).  Imagine Him
coming in His terrible Majesty, amidst the choirs of
Angels and Archangels (Matt. xxv. 31) !  In that so
terrible assize, the multitude, both of the elect and of
the reprobate, will stand before Him, and what each
separate soul hath done will be brought to light.  There,
first and foremost, will appear Peter, and the converts
of Judæa, whom he drew after him (Gal. ii. 7, 8) ; then
Paul, leading along with him, as I may truly say, the
converted world; Andrew his Achaia, John his Asia
(Rev. i. 4), Thomas his India, each one his gains to
Christ, presented, one and all, before the universal
Judge.  There, I say, will appear these rams of the
Lord's flock (Ps. lxiv. 14) with all the souls they had
severally gained to God by their holy preaching !  On
that great occasion, then, when the shepherds of Christ
shall all stand with their several flocks before the Eyes

of the Chief Pastor, what shall we wretched souls have
to say, who shall be found empty ?   We, who have had
the name of Pastors, but have no sheep to show that
have been fed by our preaching !   Here we shall have
been called by the title of Shepherds ; but there we
shall produce no sheep.

———————

# CHAPTER IV.

## ON THE CHARACTERISTICS OF ZEAL.

1. LET your zeal (St. Bern. Serm. 20 in Cant. No. 4) be kindled in your breast by charity, enlightened by knowledge, and strengthened by endurance! Let it be fervent, circumspect, invariable and not lukewarm; neither let it be lacking in discretion or in courage! "I am jealous over you," says the Apostle Paul, "with a godly jealousy" (2 Cor. xi. 2). It is the Bridegroom who is jealous for his Bride; but the friend of the Bridegroom ought not to be jealous for *her*, but for her *spouse* (cf. John iii. 29).

What saith the man that loves God (St. Aug. in Ps. xxxiv.)? "O magnify the Lord with me!" As though he would say, "I am unwilling to magnify the Lord all alone—unwilling to love Him alone, or to embrace Him alone. Let all souls embrace Him, and enjoy Him with me!" If you love Him yourself, draw all *others* to His love! Draw them to the enjoyment of Him, and say: "O magnify the Lord with me, and let us exalt His Name together!" (ibid). Get possession of as many as you can, by exhortation, by help and encouragement, by entreaty, by pleading and argument, and by giving reasons, coupled with kindness and tender

consideration ! Draw them on to love, that so, if they
magnify God, they may do so unitedly.

Those who feed the flock of Christ (St. Aug. Tract.
123 on John, No. 5) with no other intention than that
it may be theirs, not His, are convicted of loving themselves and not Christ ; or of a desire to boast, or to
domineer, or to seek gain, rather than to obey and serve,
or to please God in true charity.

To such, accordingly, those words of Christ are a
perpetual rebuke, so often pressed upon us, as they
were, in the person of Peter, " If thou lovest Me, feed
My sheep." For what else does this mean, than, as if
He had said, " If thou lovest Me, study to feed, *not
thyself, but* My sheep ; and feed them, too, not as thine,
but as *Mine*. Seek in them My glory, not thine; My
reign, not thine ; My profit, not thine !

2. Untractable sheep (St. Aug. Serm. 46 in Ezek.
xxxiv. No. 7, de Donatistis.) are apt to say, " What do
you want with us ? Why do you thus seek after us ? "
As though this were not itself the very cause of our so
doing, that they are wandering astray and perishing !
" If I am in error," they say, " if in death, what do you
want with me ? " " It is *because* you are in error," we
say, " that we desire to recover you from it ; it is *because*
you are lost, that we are anxious to find you." " But
this is just what I decline," he replies. " I *wish* to be
in error. I *wish* to be lost." " *Do* you thus desire to
err," we reply, " *Do* you really so wish to perish ? "
How much the more do I wish that you may not do so !
It is for this very reason that I am importunate with

you. For what do I hear the Apostle say? "Preach the Word;—in season and out of season" (2 Tim. iv. 2). To whom, then, is it in season? For whom out of season? In season, I answer, to them that are willing to hear; and out of season to them that are unwilling. Therefore, I am out of season to thee thyself. I venture to say it. *Thou* wouldest go astray: *thou* wouldest perish: *I* am unwilling you should; and, lastly, He too is unwilling, Who causes me to fear Him;—that is, God. If I consent to you, hear what He saith to me; hear how He reproaches me:—" Thou hast not brought again," He saith, " that which was driven away, neither hast thou sought that which was lost" (Ezek. xxxiv. 4). Do I fear *thee*, think you, more than *Him*? I fear not thee at all. I would recall the wanderer: I would seek in you that which is lost. Whether thou wilt or no, I will do it. Though the briars of the wood tear me; I will bear all straits; I will overcome all hindrances; I will put to all the strength that the God Whom I fear gives me. I will recall the wanderer, I will seek out the perishing. If, therefore, you will not that I should suffer loss, do not wander away!—do not perish!

3. If the case require it, be ready, in behalf of the character and liberty of the Church, to surrender your means to its plunderers, your good fame to contempt, your fortune to perils, and your head to the enemy's sword. It is a spectacle delightful to Angels (1 Cor. iv. 9) when a man is held up to reproach for his righteousness by the wealthy, and to contempt by the proud. The Apostle was not afraid to expose his life

to dangers on behalf of his flock. " I am in perils,"
he said, " for *your* souls " (2 Cor. xii. 15. Vulg.). Seeing
that even the Angels acknowledge themselves to be
unworthy of the Divine favours, how can you repay
Him for all the benefits which His grace hath conferred
upon you ?  For you He laid down His own Life (John
xv. 13).  Why, then, should you hesitate to lay down
your brief life for Him—frail and uncertain as it is, and
ready to be demanded of you at any moment by the law
of nature, but a life which may now be laid down by
you, if you *will*, to your own credit and advantage ?  O
that your own will may thus readily surrender now,
what *necessity* must one day extort from you, so that
what will be a debt then, which you cannot but pay,
may be a free-will offering now !  On the testimony of
the Truth, " whosoever will lose his life, the same shall
save it; and he that will save his life shall lose it "
(Matt. x. 39).  Far wiser, therefore, is it to lose it that
you may save it, than to save it only to lose it.

It is written, " Tell the people of their sins " (Isaiah
lviii. 1).  If they harden their faces, and you in consequence harden yours, you will be opposing one hardened
face to another ; and the Lord will say to you, what it
is written that He said to His Prophet Ezekiel, " I have
made thy face strong against their faces " (Ezek. iii. 8).
It is enough if you can say with the Apostle with a good
conscience, " I testify against you this day that I am
free from the blood of all men.  For I have not been
ashamed to declare unto you the whole counsel of God "
(Acts xx. 26, 27).

# CHAPTER V.

*THAT AFTER THE EXAMPLE OF THE APOSTLES WE
SHOULD LABOUR IN THE LORD'S HARVEST.*

1. BEHOLD the world is full of Clergy, never-theless in the harvests of the Lord it is rare to find a real hard worker (St. Greg. Mag. hom. 17 in Evang. cf. Matt. ix. 38). We undertake the office, but we do not fulful our task.

If (St. Chrys. de compunct. i. 6) anyone is invited to undertake any office or ministry, anxiety is at once shown by him and the question is put, whether there be any repose to be found where one has to go;—if there be an abundance of all that is necessary, and nothing is deficient of those things which the broad way requires (Matt. vii. 13). What sayest thou, O man? What are you talking about? You are called upon to "enter in at the strait gate" (ibid). Do you hesitate for such matters as repose or abundance? You are told to travel along the narrow way. Why do you plead for the broad and the wide road? Can any-thing be more inconsistent—anything worse than such perversity?

2. Your predecessors, the Apostles, were told that "the harvest is plentiful, but that the labourers are

few" (Matt. ix. 38). Fulfil your destiny! "If children, then heirs" (Rom. viii. 17). That you may prove your ancestry, watch over your charge, and do not have it said to you, through slumbering in indolence and sloth, "Why stand ye here all the day idle" (Matt. xx. 6)?

I would have you glory in this which is the best of all glories, such as the Apostles and Prophets preferred to all other;—namely, "I will rather glory in my infirmities, that the power of Christ may rest upon me" (2 Cor. xii. 9). Demonstrate, then, your inheritance in the Cross of Christ by much labour. Happy was he who could say: "I laboured more than they all" (1 Cor. xv. 10). It is a glory, but there is nothing empty in it, nothing soft, nothing of repose. If the toil frighten you, let the reward encourage you; for "every man shall receive the reward of his own labour" (1 Cor. iii. 8). Although he laboured more than all, he did not accomplish the whole task to be performed. There is abundance of room still for more and more. Go forth into the field of the Lord (Matt. xiii. 38), and consider diligently with how many thorns and thistles it is disfigured in consequence of the original curse (Gen. iii. 18). Go thy way forth into it, not as its lord, but as its husbandman, that you may see to and take care of that of which you must render an account. Go forth, then, I would say to you, with the step of an earnest anxiety, and of an anxious earnestness. For those who were bidden to go forth into the world, did not compass that world with their actual steps, so much as with their mental vision and care.

Lift up, then, as it were, the eyes of your contemplation, and behold the distant regions of the world, and see if they be not dry for the flames, rather than white for the harvest (John iv. 35). How much of what you took to be fruit, on closer inspection will turn out rather to be thorns! Nay, not thorns only, but *old trees* that will not readily bear fruit, except perchance they be acorns, or such as swine only will eat (Luke xv. 16). How long are *they* to have possession of the soil (Luke xiii. 7)? If you go forth and become aware of them, will you not be ashamed that the axe shall be idle on the ground, and that you shall have taken up the Apostolic sickle to no purpose (Mark iv. 29)?

Was it thus that the Apostles and Prophets acted? They were brave in battle (Hebr. xi. 34), not clothed in soft silks. If you are a true son of the Apostles and Prophets, be like them in action (Luke x. 37)! Vindicate your character as such by corresponding conduct: for no one is otherwise proved to be noble than by nobility of conduct, and by the courage of true faith. It is by these that men have won kingdoms, wrought righteousness, and successfully earned its promises (Hebr. xi. 33).

# CHAPTER VI.

*ST. PAUL CONSIDERED AS THE MODEL OF A GOOD PASTOR.*

1. LET us hear now what Paul himself says of Paul (St. Greg. Naz. orat. 2. de sacerd. No. 52). " In weariness and painfulness, in watchings often, in hunger and thirst, in fastings often, in cold and nakedness ; besides those things that are without, that which cometh upon me daily, the care of all the Churches. Who is weak and I am not weak? Who is offended and I burn not ? If I must needs glory, I will glory of the things which concern mine infirmities " (2 Cor. xi. 27 et sqq.). I pass by all these,—labours, watchings, fears, vexations, hunger and thirst, cold and nakedness ;—such things as came upon him from without, or troubled him from within ;—persecutions, plots, chains, accusations, courts of justice, daily and hourly perils of death, the escape in a basket from Damascus, the stonings, scourgings, lyings in wait, perils by land, perils in the sea, perils in rivers, perils among thieves, perils by his own countrymen, and perils among false brethren (2 Cor. xi. 7 et sqq.).

2. But why should I enter into more particulars ? For, living no longer to himself, but to Christ and to

His Gospel (Gal. ii. 20), and crucifying the world unto himself, and himself unto the world and to all visible things, he looked upon all things whatever as small and as unworthy of his affection ; while, at the same time, he preached the Gospel even " from Jerusalem and in all the country round about unto Illyria," was borne up into the third heaven (2 Cor. xii. 2), and beheld Paradise itself, and heard words not to be revealed.   Such was Paul, and such is everyone who is endued with his spirit.

(Further quotations on the same subject and in similar terms in the original work are for brevity's sake here omitted.   Ed.)

H

# CHAPTER VII.

---

*THAT IN PREACHING THE PRIEST SHOULD ADAPT
THE STYLE OF HIS DISCOURSE TO THE
PURPOSE OF SECURING HIS HEARERS.*

---

1. WHEN you teach publicly in the Church (St. Jerome, Ep. 34, ad Nepot. 8), it should not be your concern to secure the applause of your congregation, but rather their groans. The tears of your hearers are your most suitable praise. Your sermons should be based on the study of Scripture. I do not wish you to be a declaimer, or a mere senseless talker, but one that is well acquainted with the Mysteries of God, and with His Sacraments. To pour out rolling words, and excite the wonder of his unskilled hearers by the length of his sentences and the rapidity of his utterance, is the style of the ignorant. A bold face will sometimes support a mistaken interpretation of a text ; and, when the man who shows it has succeeded in persuading his hearers of the correctness of his statements, he imagines that he himself likewise had been in possession of a correct knowledge of his subject.

My former teacher, Gregory Nazianzen, on being asked by me what Luke meant by " the second sabbath after the first," said pleasantly, " I will answer you that

question presently in the Church ; wherein, if the congregation with one accord applaud what I shall say,
you will be compelled, against your will, either to have
learned from me what you were previously ignorant of,
or else, should you remain silent while the rest applauded,
to stand convicted of dulness of understanding." For
nothing is so easy as to deceive the vulgar and unlearned by volubility of tongue, who admire most what
they do not understand.

2. An anxious desire to be easily understood will dis-
pense with the more refined and cultivated language ;
and is not concerned for what merely sounds well, but
for what best conveys and inculcates what it is intended
to explain. He that teacheth must avoid all words
which fail to teach. And this holds true not in conversations only, whether with one person or many, but
much more before a congregation of the people, when
we must especially aim at being understood by *all alike.*
For in conversation a man is at liberty to put a question
to you ; but when all have to be silent, while you alone
are privileged to speak, and all alike are listening to
your words, no questions can be put. Nevertheless a
congregation that is anxious to hear, has ways of show-
ing whether they understand you or not ; in which case
you would do well to correct in some way the language
you have been using ; but this you cannot well do, if
you have learned your sermon by heart.

3. The preacher must understand (St. Greg. Magn.
de Cur. Past. iii. 39) that he must not exhaust the
powers of his audience, lest, so to speak, while they are

being strained too far, they be wholly broken. There are some matters which should be kept back more or less from many of your hearers, and only cautiously opened even to the few. For thus saith Wisdom Itself, " Who is that faithful and wise steward whom his Lord shall set over His household to give them their portion of meat in *due season* Luke xii. 42) ? By this word " portion," is implied the due *measure* of the word, lest, when anything is given to a heart of too small capacity to receive it, it should be rejected. Hence Paul saith : " I could not speak unto you as unto spiritual, but as unto carnal ; even as unto babes in Christ. I have fed you with milk and not with meat" (1 Cor. iii. 1). Hence also Moses, on withdrawing from his secret converse with God to meet the people, put a veil over his face which shone, so as not to display before the people the secret things of God (Exod. xxxiv. 32, 35).

# CHAPTER VIII.

*THAT PASTORS SHOULD NEVER CEASE TEACHING THE WORD OF GOD, OR IN ANY DEGREE RELAX FROM IT, ON THE SCORE OF THE OPPOSITION OF EVIL LIVERS.*

1. TO preach the Gospel is to feed the flock (St. Bern. de consid. lib. iv. c. 3. No. 6 and 8), agreeably to the office of a shepherd. " Do thou the work of an Evangelist," and thou hast fulfilled the office of the Pastor (2 Tim. iv. 5). But, you will say, " I am not better than my fathers " (1 Chron. xix. 4). Whom of them, I would ask, did the " rebellious house," I will not say, listen to, but even abstain from scorning (Ezek. ii. 5)? Do you, therefore, insist the more, in the hope that perchance they may hear and be still. " Insist," I say, albeit *they* resist. By thus speaking I may seem to say too much. But what is it but to say with Paul, " Be instant, in season and out of season " (2 Tim. iv. 2). You dare not say that the Apostle exaggerates. It was enjoined to the Prophets, " Cry aloud, spare not." But to whom, save to the wicked and to sinners? " Shew My people their wickedness, and the house of Jacob their sin " (Is. lviii. 1). Note these words, how they restrain the wicked,

and the people of God. Regard them in the same light thyself. However wicked they may be and however criminal, give heed that the Lord's words apply not to you, where He says:—" Inasmuch as ye have not done it unto the least of these My brethren, ye have not done it unto Me " (Matt. xxv. 40).

I admit that the people may have stood out hitherto with a brazen face and an unconquered heart; but that it be unconquerable, I doubt if you can venture to say you know. It may yet become, what it has not yet been. If you doubt it, yet " with God nothing is impossible " (Luke i. 37). If their faces are hardened, harden yours. There is nothing so hard but it will yield to what is harder than itself. What saith the Lord to His Prophet ? " I have given thy forehead to be harder than their foreheads " (Ezek. iii. 8).

2. Jericho is a type of this world (St. Aug. Serm. 35. Appendix ;—otherwise called " De Tempore," 106. 5. Apocr.). For if at the sound of the Trumpets its walls fell down ( Josh. vi. 20), so also now it must be that the city of the world,—that is, its pride—together with its towers,—that is, its avarice, its envy, and its luxury; along with all its inhabitants—that is to say, all evil desires—shall be destroyed and laid waste by the persistent preaching of the Priests. It is not becoming, therefore, that the Priest should be silent in the Church (1 Cor. xiv. 34), but that he should give heed to what the Lord saith, " Cry aloud; spare not; lift up thy voice like a trumpet, and tell My people of their sins " (Is. lviii. 1). We are commanded, then, you perceive,

to " cry," and " to cry aloud."   " Spare not," He saith ;
that is, spare not the iniquity of the sinner, lest you
perish by your own silence, and, while you consult his
feelings, neglect to consult his health.   Do not by your
silence let his wounds grow worse, which you might
have healed by lifting up your voice.   We are bidden
therefore to " cry ; " and that no one should be able to
say that he did not hear, or that the voice of the Priest
had failed to reach this person or that, we are bidden
to " cry *aloud ;* " and if even this should not suffice for
the purpose, He goes on to say, " Lift up thy voice like
a *trumpet.*"

A trumpet, then, we see, is necessary to reach the
ears of sinners, such as shall not enter into their ears
alone, but shall make their very hearts tremble, stirring
up the servant to good works, and striking terror into
the hearts of the wicked for their sins.   For as, in a
battle, the trumpet casts down the heart of the timid
soldier, while it kindles the courage of the brave, so
the trumpet of the Priest humbles the soul of the
sinner and strengthens the spirit of the virtuous ; and
thus with one and the same sound he gives exhortation
to the one to be stronger for the fight, while he fills the
other with fear, that he may be less forward to sin.

Lastly, at the sound of the trumpets of the Priests
the walls of Jericho, which held within them the sinful
people, fell down.   No ram struck them, no engine of
war was brought against them, but what is most wonderful, the *sound of the Priests' trumpets,* as by a kind of
terror, alone overthrew them.   But that all these things

were done in a figure (1 Cor. x. 6), there can be no
doubt. For what else do we believe to have been pre-
figured by the trumpets of the Priests of that period,
than the preaching of the Priests of this; by which
they cease not to announce by their terrible sound the
just judgment which will fall upon all sinners, to warn
them of the fearful death of hell, and to smite the ears
of their delinquent flocks with the stern language of
threatening? For as the shrill sound of the trumpets
on that occasion threw down the walls of cement and
reached the ears of the people who were enclosed within
them, so now the preaching of the Priests, throwing
down the depraved imaginations behind which men
hide themselves, penetrates to their very inmost souls
*(animæ nudæ)*; and as, then, the sound of the Divine
Voice destroyed and took captive that obstinate and
stubborn people, so now the preaching of the Priests
brings sinners into subjection.

The ordained preachers of the Gospel are these
trumpets of *beaten* silver (cf. Numbers x. 2), which by
their constant bruisings which they receive at the
hands of the world, and by the manifold and bitter
sufferings which fall to their lot, are so much the more
advanced in the love of God. The trumpets are of
silver, because the teachers of the people ought to be
well instructed in the word of God, that they may not
be found ignorant in their duty of teaching what they
would have the people do, as David saith:—" The
words of the Lord are pure words; even as silver is
tried in the fire" (Ps. xii. 6).

# CHAPTER IX.

*THAT WE SHOULD PRACTISE BEFORE WE PREACH.*

1. THE Baptism of Christ (Greg. Naz. Orat. 39 in Sancta lumina No. 14) ought to be a lesson to us that the cleansing and humiliation of the soul should first take place in ourselves, and that we ought not to undertake the work of preaching till we have first, as it were, come of age, both in the bodily and in the spiritual sense of those words (Luke iii. 23). We see that Moses (Greg. Nyss. de vitâ Moysis, 196), before he had attained to the most perfect degree of virtue, was unable even to reconcile two men (Exod. ii. 14); whilst at a subsequent period, after he had spent a considerable time at leisure and alone, he was readily welcomed by many thousands (Exod. iv. 31). Thus the authority of Holy Scripture is seen to declare, as with a loud voice, that men must not assume too hastily the position of public teachers, and not until by great diligence and considerable labour they shall have earned that degree of authority over others which shall lead men to consent readily to their teaching.

2. Of what sort, then, ought they to be (St. Basil, Ex. mor. regul. 80. c. 12 to 22. " Theses collectæ ") to whom

the preaching of the Gospel is entrusted? I answer, they ought to be as the Apostles and Ministers of Christ and the faithful dispensers of the Mysteries of God (1 Cor. iv. 1); discharging those duties which God hath prescribed to them to the utmost of their ability both in word and in deed;—as the heralds of the kingdom of Heaven (Luke x. 11), to the destruction of him who holds the empire of death through sin;—as the pattern and example of true piety, that all men who follow the Lord may be directed by them into the ways of uprightness, and that the obstinacy of those may be exposed, who in any way resist His authority:—as the eye in the body, that they may discern between the good and the evil, and assign to each man, as to the members of Christ, the duties suitable to his calling:—as the shepherds of the flock of Christ, who, as occasion may require, may be ready even to lay down their own lives for the sheep, that they may impart to them the Gospel of Christ (John x. 11):—as physicians of the soul, who shall with the utmost gentleness, and with fidelity to the doctrine of the Lord, cure the diseases of men's souls (1 Thess. v. 9), and restore them to the healthy vigour and perseverance which is in Christ:—as the parents or other relatives and nurses of children (1 Thess. ii. 7), who, in the greatness of their affection for them in Christ, are ready not only to preach to them the Gospel of Christ, but even to lay down their own lives on their behalf:—as the helpers of God, who, by deeds that are alone worthy of God, devote themselves entirely to His glory:—and lastly, as the builders of the Temple of God (I Cor. iii. 10), who so prepare and make ready the soul of each separate person, that it shall be exactly fitted to the foundation of the Apostles and Prophets (Eph. ii. 21).

3. The man who by necessity of his calling (St. Greg. Mag. Ep. 25 ad Joan : Ep. Const. i. 9) is compelled to speak on the highest of all subjects, is compelled also by the like necessity to illustrate the same in his life. For that voice will the more readily penetrate the hearts of his hearers, which the life of the speaker teaches by its practical example. For what he teaches by word, he does by his example promote in the practice of those who hear him. Hence it is said by the Prophet : " Get ye up into the *high mountain*, ye that preach the Gospel to *Z*ion" (Is. xl. 9) ; signifying thereby that the man who applies himself to the preaching of heavenly things, should forsake the grovelling occupations of this lower world, and shew himself as standing on the level of the loftiest subjects, and thus so much the more easily draw his hearers on to better things, as it is by the meritoriousness of his life that he thus truly proclaims them from above (John viii. 23).

# CHAPTER X.

---

*THAT PRAYER AND TRUE PIETY ADD FORCE AND EFFECT TO PREACHING.*

---

1. A LIVING and most effectual sermon, indeed (St. Bernard, Ep. ad Bald. Abbot), is preached by the example of good conduct itself alone, as giving practical effect to that which is taught, through demonstrating the possibility of what is urged. Understand, therefore, that on these instructions of mine, as regards *preaching* and setting a good *example* at the same time, hangs the whole sum and substance of your office for the security of your conscience therein.

But, if you are wise, you will add yet another, and that is the diligent habit of *prayer*, so as to satisfy the three-fold requirements of that three-fold injunction of the Lord to Peter to feed His sheep. You will know that the Sacrament of this three-fold charge will have been in no way frustrated by you, if you feed the flock of the Lord by the Word, by your own good example, and by the fruits of holy prayer. There remain, therefore, these three things that I have named, the Word, your own example, and Prayer: but the greatest of these is Prayer. For although it is the work that gives force to the voice (Ps. lxviii. 33), nevertheless, both for the work and for the voice alike, it is prayer that secures the efficacy of Divine grace.

The Lord Jesus (St. Ambr. in Ps. cxix., Serm. 20, No. 24) did not continue all night in prayer, as one who could in no *other* way reconcile His Father to us; but to show what were the qualifications of a faithful advocate, and what those of a Priest;—namely, that he should plead in prayer for the flock of Christ, not by day only, but by night.

2. Let not the Priest doubt for a moment that he will advance himself more by the pious exercise of prayer than by the facility of preaching (St. Aug. de doct. Chr. lib. iv. 15. No. 32), and that by praying both for himself and for those whom he is about to address, he should make himself a pray-er before he becomes a preacher. At the very time that he is about to preach, before he opens his lips, let him lift up his thirsting heart to God, that he may utter that which has been put into his mouth by Him (Ps. cxix. 171), and pour forth effectually that with which it has been filled. For when the time comes that there are many things to be said, and many ways in which they *may* be said concerning the matters of faith and charity, who is there that knows so well what it is which at this particular time it is expedient for us to say, or for our flocks to hear, as He Who seeth the hearts of all? And who is it that causeth us to say what ought to be said, and *that* in the manner in which it *ought* to be said, save He in Whose Hands are both we ourselves and our utterances (Wisd. vii. 16)?

But whether the Priest is about to speak to the people generally or to a single individual (St. Aug. de doct. Christ. lib. iv. 30, 63), let him in either case pray that God will put good words into his mouth. For if Queen Esther prayed, when about to speak to the king on behalf of the temporal safety of her people, that God would put into her mouth words suitable to her purpose (Esther iv. 16), how much more ought he to pray for the same gift, who labours both in word and doctrine for the eternal salvation of men (1 Tim. v. 17)?

Do not fancy that any one among men will learn anything from a mere fellow man (St. Aug. Tract. 3 in Ep. i. John, No. 13). We can admonish them by the tones of our natural voice; but it is the Master Who teaches (Matt. xxiii. 10). Christ teaches. His inspiration it is which teaches. Where His inspiration and unction are absent, our words issue from our lips in vain (1 John ii. 27).

# CHAPTER XI.

*THAT THE PRIEST SHOULD ESCHEW ENVY, AS THE*
*MOST TO BE ABHORRED OF ALL VICES.*

1. THERE are many (St. Chrys. in Ep. ad Rom. hom. vii. No. 5) who weep with them that weep, and are not unwilling to rejoice with them that do rejoice (Rom. xii. 15), while with some that rejoice they nevertheless lament, which comes of ill-will and spleen. They will endure to do what is somewhat troublesome, while they will neglect to do what is comparatively light and easy; and they waste away and perish when they see others prosperous and successful, nay, when they see the whole Church, whether in word or in any other matter, happy and flourishing. And what can be worse than this? For such an one does not fight against his brother only, but against God. Nay, he may be more harmful than even Satan himself; for we can beware of Satan, but men like these, bearing the mask of friendship, kindle a flame secretly, and cast themselves first into the fire, and are oppressed with troubles, which not only excite in others no pity, but, on the contrary rather derision.

2. Why do you grow pale, I ask, and tremble and are afraid? What is the matter with you? Is it because

a brother is illustrious, distinguished and approved?
Ought you not to don a crown and rejoice and give
glory to God that a member of your body is illustrious
and glorious? Instead of that, you are sad and
depressed because God is glorified. Do you not see
whither such hostile feelings may lead you? But you
will say, "I am not grieved because God is glorified, but
because my brother Priest is." But what is the consequence? That God is glorified in him, and you are
irritated. Nay, you will say, it is not this that displeases
me, but I should like God to be glorified through me
*also*. Rejoice, then, in the success of thy brother, and
God *will* be glorified in thee too; and all men will say,
" Blessed be God, Who has such servants, so free from
all feelings of envy, and rejoicing in one another's
prosperity!" But why do I call him your brother? For,
even if he were your enemy and not your friend, and
God were glorified by his means, on that very account
it would become you to regard him as your friend. It
is you who make him your enemy, who is in truth your
friend, seeing that God is glorified in him by his
distinguished conduct (Matt. v. 16). How could you
more conspicuously wage war against Christ than by
such behaviour as this?

Though a man should work miracles, practise con-
tinence and fasting, lie on the bare ground, and attain
by such methods as these even to Angelic virtue, if he
were troubled with but this one vice, he would be the
basest of all men—baser than the adulterer, or the
fornicator, or the thief.

# CHAPTER XII.

*THAT IT IS OUR DUTY TO INSTRUCT THE YOUNGER
AND MORE UNLEARNED OF OUR HEARERS
WITH A GENTLE AND READY MIND.*

1. THERE are many (St. Aug. Serm. xlvii. de
ovibus in Ezek. xxxiv. 8. No. 9. Compare
also St. Greg. de cur, past. 1, 2) who learn
with composed minds, but teach with impetuosity (cf.
Ezek. xxxiv. 18, 19) ; and, although they have a patient
Teacher for themselves, behave impatiently and roughly
towards their own disciples. We all know how gently
the Scriptures teach us, A man comes to them accordingly, and reads in them the Commandments of God.
He reads, and he bears in mind what he reads. He
admits into his soul in tranquillity what he reads of that
which is in itself tranquil. But if someone comes to
hear about it from him, he is angry and disquieted ;
accusing his hearer at one time of slowness, at another
of stupidity ; and thus, through causing him distress
of mind, prevents him from understanding properly
what, in a more composed condition, he might readily
have listened to and remembered. I do not, however,
say this, as if there were never cases in which stupidity
must be corrected—such as the notable tranquillity of

I

the Truth Himself corrects, where He saith, " O ye
fools and slow of heart to believe " (Luke xxiv. 25)—
provided, however, we do it with the loving intention
of exciting necessary carefulness and concern in the
minds of our hearers, so as to quicken their purpose
of heart, and to remove those clouds from their minds
with which the concerns of this lower world have en-
compassed them.    Such teachers as these, therefore,
are not to be blamed ; but only such as do so in bitterness and in ill-will ; men of a sour temper, and ill-
conditioned—not in body, but in mind.

2. If we are studious (St. Aug. Catech. rud. xii. 17) to
repeat over and over again common-place truths, and
such as are suitable to children, we shall adapt ourselves
to them with a brotherly, fatherly, and even motherly
love ; and, heart being knit to heart, we shall come to
discern even things new to ourselves.    For such is the
power of sympathetic minds, that while our hearers on
their part, are influenced by our works, we ourselves
become, as it were, domiciled *(habitamus)* with them,
and so both they who hear will, as it were, speak in us,
and we shall learn from them how to teach them.

# CHAPTER XIII.

*THAT THE PREACHER SHOULD PREFER THE HORTATORY TO THE ARGUMENTATIVE STYLE.*

1. **W**HAT Paul saith to his disciple Timothy (St. Greg. Mag. Moral. in Job xxiii. 7), "These things teach and exhort with all authority," was not designed to promote a domineering power over others, but the influence of a good life. For when the conscience causes the tongue to hesitate, confidence ceases to be placed in its teaching. Hence it was not the influence of an exalted style which the Apostle would suggest, but that which is due to the confidence men place in a good life. Hence it is written also concerning the Lord, "He taught them as one having authority, and not as the scribes" (Matt. vii. 29 and Acts i. 1). For, in a manner peculiar to Himself, and with authority, He alone spake the truth with power; seeing that He fell into no errors of life through infirmity. For it was through His Divine Nature that He possessed in Himself what He ministered to us by the innocence of His Life.

We, then, who are but weak mortals, when we speak about God to men, must first bear in mind what we are ourselves, that we may judge rightly from our own infirmity by what sort of instruction we shall best consult the interests of our people.   Let us consider, therefore, whether we are not such as we blame some others for being, or whether we ever were such—although by the grace of God, we be not such *now*—that so we may learn to correct them the more gently, in proportion as we see ourselves, as it were, *in* them.   And, even if we are not such, and never were such, let us beware that our heart be not lifted up, and our very innocence be a snare to us; and let us set against the evils of those whom we are correcting the good points we may observe them to possess.   And if there be none such, let our minds take refuge in the secret judgment of God, as remembering that whatever good there may be in ourselves we have received from Him, and that His grace may yet abundantly descend upon these also, as it has upon ourselves, so that they may come even to surpass us in goodness.   Who would have believed that Saul would ever have come to surpass Stephen by the merit of the Apostleship, who held the clothes of them that stoned him ?   With these thoughts, then, let the Priest study to keep his conscience humble and tender, before he rebukes others for their delinquencies !

2. These are suitable thoughts for all such Priests (Greg. Mag. Mor. in Job xxi. 9) as are disposed to be over-severe to their hearers, in preference to dealing kindly with them.   Such Priests as these are over-anxious to appear to them as their superiors, and take more pleasure in dealing harshly with them than gently. Of such it is written, " The rod of pride is in the mouth

of a fool " (Prov. xiv. 3) ; because he knows how to strike severely, but cannot compassionate humbly.

3. Many Priests, nevertheless, are guilty of this fault, and hence it is written, " The words of the wise are as goads, and as nails fastened by the Masters of assemblies, which are given from one Shepherd " (Eccles. xii. 11). And were not the words of Paul as goads, when he said :—" O foolish Galatians, who hath bewitched you" (Gal. iii. 1) ? And again to the Corinthians, " So long as there is envy and strife among you, are ye not carnal and walk as men " (1 Cor. iii. 3) ? But we should not fail to observe the care which these holy teachers take, and the diligence with which they search for grounds of approval and praise, before descending to correction and blame.

## CHAPTER XIV.

*THAT PASTORS OUGHT TO BE MORE PROFICIENT IN*
*GENTLENESS THAN IN HARSHNESS.*

1. IT is not by roughness (St. Aug. Ep. xxii. ad Aurel. Episc. No. 5) nor by harshness, nor by an imperious manner that vices are, for the most part, overcome. It is mostly by teaching rather than by commanding, by warning rather than by threatening that this is done. For it is no more possible to please men without gentleness, than it is to please God without faith (St. Bern. Serm. 5, in vigil : Nat. Dom, No. 4). Our Lord Jesus Christ (St. Cyril Alex. lib. iii. t. 1. in Is. xxvi. 9, 10), having cast forth the net of gentleness, has caught, as it were, the whole world in its delicate meshes.

Learn then (St. Bernard, Serm. 23 in Cant. No. 2), that you should be as the tender mothers of your flocks, not as their lords. Study rather to be loved than to be feared. And if sometimes there be need of severity, let it be paternal, not tyrannical. Show yourselves as mothers in cherishing, and as fathers in correcting. Be gentle. Put all fierceness aside. Forbear the scourge. Let your breasts, indeed, abound with milk, but not be swollen with it ; why overload them with *your* burden, whose burdens you yourself ought to be bearing (cf. Acts. xv. 10)? Why should the child that has been bitten by a serpent dread to make it known to the physician, to whom it were more fitting that it should at once resort, as to its own mother's breast? If you are spiritual, instruct such as these in the spirit of gentleness; "considering thyself lest thou also be tempted" (Gal. vi. 1). If you fail in this matter, he will die in his sin; but "his blood," saith the Lord, "I will require at your hands" (Ezek. iii. 18).

2. Nothing more effectually tests a spiritual man (St. Aug. in Ep. ad Gal. vi. No. 56) than his treatment of *another's sins ;*—when he studies his *deliverance* from them rather than their abounding in him, and his *relief* under their weight rather than his punishment for them; and, as far as in him lies, undertakes to effect it. Hence the Apostle says again :—" If any man be overtaken in a fault, let them that are spiritual among you restore such an one in the spirit of *meekness* " (Gal. vi. 1); and then, lest anyone should fancy himself to be restoring his brother, while in fact he is recklessly provoking him, and deriding him for his faults, or else, haughtily testifying against him as incurable, he adds, " Considering *thyself*, lest thou also be tempted " (ibid). For nothing inclines a man so much to mercy and pity as the thought of his *own* danger.

" Depart from us," says the haughty Priest (St. Jerome, lib. ii. in Lam. Jerem. iv. 15. Apoc.). Do not trouble us with your communications :—your wounds are incurable. Such talk as this will enlighten none that are blind and heal none that are sick, nay, will rather slay them and drive them into the perilous condition of despair. Good pastors, judging of their own infirmities from those of other men, will study rather to deliver others out of the net of error by the humility and gentleness of their treatment, than to send them by an austere manner into the pit of perdition.

3. Anyone who conceals his own sins (St. Prosp. De vitâ contemplativâ et activâ ii. 16. Apocr.), which he ought to be conscious of and to lament, will go on doing so to his injury, so long as he dwells too curiously upon the sins of others. But if, *looking into his own heart*, he studies his own manner of life, he is no longer over-careful to reprehend the sins of others, but rather to lament his own. We ought not to be over-ready to discern the faults of others and to condemn them, but rather, when we do see them, so to lament them that by "bearing one another's burdens we may so fulfil the law of Christ" (Gal. vi.' 2); for *He* rather "*bore* our sins" than *accused* us of them, as the Evangelist writes: "Behold the Lamb of God Which *taketh away* the sins of the world" (John i. 29)! If, therefore, He Who was without sin (John viii. 7 and 46) supported, and will continue to support, us sinners by His unspeakable affection, "not desiring that any should perish, but that all should come to repentance," nor that sinners should die, but rather that they should live (2 Pet. iii. 9), why should not we, after the example of our Lord and Saviour, "support the weak" (1 Thess. v. 14), when we ourselves are either sick and having need to be sup-

ported by God, or, if we be sound, may yet in our frailty come to be sick ?

Bear thou, then, with others, seeing that in all probability thou thyself art being borne with (St. Aug. Serm. xlvii. de ovibus, in Ezek. xxxiv. No. 5). If you have been *always* good, have the *more* compassion on others. If on the contrary you have at any time been otherwise, *do not forget the fact.* But *who* is there that has been always good ? Probably, if God were to search thee diligently, He would find thee even now evil, whom thou thyself hast always found good. But, be it otherwise, will you, because you have swift feet for passing over the bridge, on that account cut it down for others?

4. Preserve thou to me, O Lord, that which has been Thine own gift (St. Ambr. de penit. ii. 8. 73 et sqq). Guard the gift which Thou bestowedst upon me even whilst I fled from it ; nor suffer the lost one whom Thou calledst to the Priesthood to perish as a Priest ? Grant me Thy grace that I may know how to comfort the sinner with heartfelt concern ! For this is the height of virtue :—as it is written, " Thou shouldest not have rejoiced over the children of Judah in the day of their destruction ; nor spoken proudly in the day of their distress (Obadiah 12, 13). As often, then, as the sin of anyone that has fallen has been exposed, let me compassionate him, and not haughtily reproach him, but mourn and lament over him; and whilst I do so, mourn at the same time over myself and say, " Tamar is more righteous than I " (Gen. xxxviii. 26).

Possibly some young woman of your flock may have

fallen. She may have been deceived and led into sin by the occasions which are the ordinary encouragement to such falls. We all of us fall, even we who are older. " The law of the flesh warreth against the law of the mind, and leads us into sin, so that we do what we would not " (Rom. vii. 23). Youth affords some excuse for her, which it does not for me ; for it is her place to learn—ours to teach. Hence, again, " Tamar is more righteous than I."

We accuse another of avarice : let us call to mind if we ourselves have been guilty of avarice ; and, if so, seeing that " avarice is the root of all evil " (1 Tim. vi. 10), and spreads as it were underground secretly in our whole body, let everyone of us say to ourselves, " Tamar is more righteous than I." For if we thus speak to ourselves, it is a means of our having such a care of ourselves, that the Lord Jesus shall not say concerning us, " Thou beholdest the mote that is in thy brother's eye, but seest not the beam which is in thine own eye. Thou hypocrite, first cast out the beam out of thine own eye, and then shalt thou see clearly to cast out the mote out of thy brother's eye " (Matt. vii. 4, 5).

## CHAPTER XV.

*THAT IT IS THE DUTY OF A GOOD PASTOR TO BE
LIBERAL TO THE POOR.*

1. IT is one of our first duties (St. Greg. Mag. hom. 14 in Evang. De bonis pastoribus. init.) not only to be liberal to Christ's poor (2 Cor. xii. 15); but after that, if needful, even to lay down our own lives for them (John x. 11). But it is from the former that we arrive by degrees to the latter. But, seeing that the soul whereby we live is incomparably superior to the earthly material which is gathered around it, the man who does not give his substance to the sheep, is scarcely to be found giving his *life* for them. And there are some, who, whilst loving their earthly substance more than their flocks, deservedly forfeit the name of shepherds;—as the Lord saith, " The hireling, who is not the shepherd of the sheep "—not he to whom the sheep belong—" seeth the wolf coming, and leaveth the sheep, and fleeth " (John x. 12). And that Pastor is rightly called an hireling, who feeds the sheep, not from any personal love that he has for them, but with an eye to temporal gain.

A discourse cannot penetrate the mind of one who is deficient in learning (St. Greg. Mag. de cur. past. ii. 7), where the hand of pity and generosity does not commend the preacher to the hearer. But the seed sown will soon take root and prosper in his heart, where the kindly affection of the preacher duly waters it. Hence it follows (St. Greg. Mag. Ep. xxx. 6. 14) that he must not fancy that reading and praying only will suffice to produce this effect, while he aims at keeping at a distance, and hopes to prosper with a closed hand. On the contrary let him be liberal; let him meet the necessities of those who suffer (Eph. iv. 28), and regard their wants as if they were his own; for, while he is devoid of these qualifications, he has but an empty name.

2. The man has always something to give (St. Bernard in Ps. xxxvi.) who has a heart abounding with charity. Let him therefore give cheerfully what he can afford, whether to their carnal necessities or to their spiritual, and he will erect a fortress against the Devil in the hearts of the faithful; for " The Lord loveth a cheerful giver" (2 Cor. ix. 7). Let him not, then, be overcome by weariness under difficult circumstances which cannot be avoided, that it may be made manifest to men that he is himself but a man. Let no anger be displayed towards anyone who might behave violently towards him, or beg importunately of him when compelled by circumstances, or who troubles him with his concerns when he is otherwise and more seriously engaged.

3. I know that most priests (St. Ambr. de off. Min. lib. ii. 16. 78) the more they give, the more they abound in the means of giving; seeing that whosoever recognizes

in him a faithful steward, will readily confide to his care what he would bestow upon the poor, in the assurance that his offerings will duly reach them.

To rob a friend of anything is theft (St. Jerome, Ep. 34 ad Nepot. 16) :—to defraud the Church is sacrilege ;— to have received what was designed for the poor and the hungry, and to be chary in its distribution, or timid, or, what is still more blameable, to appropriate any of it to one's self, surpasses the cruelty of every sort of thief. I am tormented with hunger, and you measure out according to your own judgment how much is sufficient for me! Either distribute at once what you have received, or, if you are a timid dispenser, return it to the giver to do so for himself.

---

## CHAPTER I.

*IT IS BETTER FOR A PRIEST TO HAVE A CARE
FOR THE SOULS OF HIS FLOCK, THAN TO BE
ENGAGED IN MERE TEMPORAL THINGS.*

1. THE Pastor of a parish (Greg. Mag. de cur. past. ii. 7) should not diminish aught of his concern for things spiritual in order to give himself to external matters, nor yet altogether neglect outward things in his attention to things inward, lest he should come to neglect one or the other in matters of interest to his flock. For it often happens that Priests, forgetting that their call is to attend to the concerns of souls, devote themselves too exclusively to external matters, are pleased with them whenever they are to be had, and miss them when they are not; so that when, as circumstances arise, they are relieved of these, they are distressed at their want of occupation. For they regard it as a pleasure, if they are burdened with these secular matters, and a burden if they are not; and thus it follows that while they delight in being occupied busily in these temporal concerns, they remain ignorant of what they ought to be teaching their flocks.

Hence, as a matter of course, the spiritual life of

their flocks grows torpid; because, albeit it craves to be maintained in vigour, it stumbles, as it were, at the example of the Priest, as at some obstacle in their way. For when the head is sick, it is to no purpose that the members are strong, and an army follows to no purpose after a missing enemy, if led astray by the General himself. There is no exhortation to lift up the hearts of the flock, and no rebuke to correct their faults.

2. We bear with more indifference the losses of Christ, than we do our own (St. Bern. de consid. lib. iv. c. 6. 20). We keep our daily accounts with care, taking no account all the while of the losses sustained by the Lord's flock. About the cost of our victuals and the number of our loaves, there is a daily reckoning with our servants, but it is rarely that we take account of the sins of our people. An ass stumbles and falls, and there is some one at once to pick her up again; but a soul perishes, and no one cares about it (Isaiah lvii. 1). And no wonder, when we take no notice even of our own falls! In examining our accounts we are distressed and anxious. Should we lament the loss of our goods more than that of our souls? "Why," asks the Apostle, "do you not suffer yourselves (even) to be defrauded" (1 Cor. vi. 7)?

You who are set to teach others, teach yourself, I pray you, if you have not already done so, to account your soul of more value than your goods. These transitory things, which can be of no real value to you, let them go from you, rather than take possession of you. Where the river flows, it wears away the ground; and just so the stream of temporal concerns wears away the conscience. If the torrent can rush over the field without injuring the crops, then may you safely handle these earthly matters without any injury to your souls.

3. A certain wise man (St. Greg. de curâ past. i. 4) says well :—" My son, meddle not with many matters " (Eccles. xi. 10); and he says so, because it is plain that the mind cannot be gathered up into the pursuit of any one matter, while it is distracted by many. When it is drawn aside by excessive care, it comes to neglect its proper concerns, frets over external matters, and becomes ignorant of itself most of all. While occupied about a multitude of things, and, knowing nothing as it ought to know, it is like one that is engaged in a journey and forgets the road. In this way he forsakes the study of himself and observes not his losses, nor in how many matters he fails.

4. He, then, is not wise, who is not wise to himself (Prov. ix. 12). A wise man will be wise to himself, and will be the first to draw water out of his own well. Let your consideration of yourself proceed *from* yourself; yet not so only, but let it end *in* yourself; and whithersoever it may wander, recall it to yourself with the good fruit of salvation. Let yourself be the first and the last in this consideration. Take for your example the great Father of all, Who sent forth His Word, *yet still retained Him. Your* "word" is your consideration of yourself, which if it go forth from you, let it not depart altogether. So let it proceed from you, as not to *escape* from you; so let it go forth, as not to *desert*.

## CHAPTER II.

*RECOMMENDING HUMILITY, AND ITS SPECIAL POWER
IN THE CHARACTER OF THE PASTOR.*

1. THE best foundation of all is humility (St. Bern. De consid. lib. ii. 6. 13), whereon if the whole spiritual building be constructed, it grows into an Holy Temple in the Lord (Eph. ii. 21). By the power of this grace alone some have gained possession even of the very gates of the enemy (Gen. xxii. 17, &c.). For what virtue is there that can more successfully wage war against the pride of the Devil or the tyranny of men ? But while this grace is, as it were, a tower of strength against the face of the enemy to every one alike (Ps. lxi. 3), I know not how much greater is its power in the case of the great, or more conspicuous in the case of the illustrious among men ; and there can be no more magnificent jewel than it in the adornment of the highest functionaries of the Church.

2. Let the Priest, then, be unceasingly studious (St. Greg. Mag. de cur. past. ii. 6) that his authority, however lofty it may seem to be in its outward exercise, may be so much the more lowered in his own estimation, that it do not get the mastery of his soul, nor

K

carry it away with such excessive self-congratulation, that he cannot keep it in due subjection through his love of power.    That this may not be the result, it is well said by a certain wise man :—" If thou be made the master of a feast, lift not thyself up, but be among them as one of the rest " (Ecclus. xxxii. 1).    Hence also Peter saith, " Neither being as lords over God's heritage, but being examples to the flock " (1 Pet. v. 3). Hence also the Truth Himself, stirring us up to seek the loftier heights of virtue, saith, " Know ye not that the Princes of the Gentiles bear rule over them, and they that are great exercise authority upon them?    But it shall not be so among you ; but whosover will be great among you, let him be your minister, and he that will be greatest among you, let him be your servant. For the Son of Man came not to be ministered unto, but to minister " (Matt. xx. 25, et seq.).    Hence it follows that the servant who is puffed up with the authority which his office confers upon him, is warned of the punishment which awaits him ; as the Lord here adds :—" But if that evil servant shall say in his heart, ' My Lord delayeth His coming,' and shall begin to smite his fellow-servants, and to eat and drink with the drunken, the Lord of that servant will come in a day that he thinketh not, and in an hour that he knoweth not of, and will cut him asunder and assign him his portion with the hypocrites " (Luke xii. 45, et seq.).    For it is among the hypocrites that the man shall deservedly receive his portion, who under the semblance of discipline turns the ministry of the Priesthood into a mere domineering power.

3. It must also be understood (St. Greg. Mag. de cur. past. ii. 8) that good Priests should not be anxious to please men, but that they should, by the respect they gain from them, lead their flocks to the love of the Truth. Not that they should desire to be loved for their own sakes, but that they should turn the affection that is felt for them into the love of Him Who is their Creator; for it is difficult for a preacher who is not loved, to obtain a ready hearing, however justly he may denounce the faults of his flock. The man, therefore, who occupies the place of eminence, should study to be loved that he may be listened to ; and yet, at the same time, not seek their love for his own sake, lest he be found secretly to be tyrannizing over those whom he seems to be serving agreeably to his sacred office. This Paul insinuates, where he sets forth the extent of his love for us, saying :—" Even as I please all men in all things " (1 Cor. x. 33) ; who nevertheless says again :—" If I were to please men, I should not be the servant of Christ " (Gal. i. 10). Paul, therefore, we see, both pleases and refuses to please ; seeing that in whatsoever respect he desires to please, he seeks not that he, personally, should please them, but the Truth by his means (cf. St. Aug. Serm. xvii. de ovibus, on Ezek. xxxiv. 9).

# CHAPTER III.

*THAT PRIESTS SHOULD NOT BE IDLE, BUT DEVOTE THEMSELVES TO SACRED STUDIES.*

1. ALTHOUGH the wise man says rightly that wisdom is the fruit of leisure (Eccles. xxxviii. 15), we must not forget that another fruit of leisure is idleness (St. Bernard de consid. lib. ii. 13. No. 22). All leisure, therefore, must not be regarded as the natural parent of trifling, but as the foster-mother of virtues. Be always occupied, therefore, in some good work or other, that the Devil may never find you *idling* (Matt. xii. 44).

If you have a servant (St. Chrys. hom. 16 in Eph. No. 1) who, although he may not rob you, nor assault you, nor contradict you, nor be drunken, nor be guilty of any like faults, nevertheless sits all day doing nothing, would you not scourge him as a good-for-nothing idler?

It is surely lawful, they say (St. Chrys. hom. 16 in Ephes. No. 7), to tell stories to pass away the time. To pass away the time, do you say? The time given you for repentance, for the acquirement of grace and for the promotion of glory, and which the Creator has granted you for these purposes? Surely not!

Why, I would ask (St. Ambr. de off. min. lib. 1, ch.

20. No. 88), do you not spend your leisure time in reading? Why not wait upon Christ, converse with Christ, listen to Christ? We address Him when we pray. We hear Him when we read His Words. What have we to do in other people's houses? There is one house in which there is room for all. There would they prefer to find us, who desire to confer with us.* What have we to do with stories? We have received the Ministry of the Altars of Christ, not the compliance with men's desires and habits for our occupation.

2. Consider, then (St. Jerome, Comm. in Haggai ii. 12), that it is the business of the Priest to answer the people's questions about Holy Scriptures. If he be a Priest, let him study the law of God. If he knows it not, he declares himself to be no Priest. For it is the Priest's office to expound the Scriptures to his people. That which we read in Deuteronomy (xvii. 8), that, when any disputes had arisen in the cities of Israel between blood and blood, or between judgment and judgment, or between leprous and leprous and between any disputing parties, they should go to the Priests and Levites, and to the High Priest, who should be in office in those days, and inquire of them the law of the Lord, and that on their answering them, they should abide by their judgments; and if they did not do so, they should be put away from among the congregation. But this rule does not belong to the Old Testament alone;

---

* The translator would gladly call the attention of the Clergy to these words, and suggest to them the custom, usefully adopted by some, of being accessible in the Church, at least at fixed convenient hours, and that the Church itself should always be so accessible.

for the Apostle says to Timothy that a Bishop ought not only to be blameless, and the husband of one wife, and wise, and modest, and accomplished and hospitable, but also a *teacher of the people* (1 Tim. iii. 2). Thus we learn from both testaments alike that it is the office of the Priests to make themselves acquainted with the law of God, and to answer the questions of the people ; and not to content themselves with mere abstinence and moderation in diet, unless they also teach the same to the people committed to their charge (cf. Deut. xvii. 10 and Mal. ii. 17).

3. How can a man be excused ignorance, who professes to teach others ? " If a man be ignorant, he will be ignored " (*ignorabitur*. 1 Cor. xiv. 38, vulg.), and will make others ignorant too. How dangerous it is for the shepherd to provide no pasture, for the guide to be ignorant of the road, and for the Priest to be ignorant of His Lord's Will, the Church has daily experience. For the Will of God, as it is most holy, so is it also a very secret thing, and altogether an occult counsel— one of which the Apostle boasts, where he says : " I think also that I have the Spirit of God " (1 Cor. vii. 40). Hence also the Truth Himself saith (by His Apostle) : " No man knoweth what is in man, save the spirit of the man which is in him. So no man knoweth the things which are of God, save the Spirit of God which is in him " (1 Cor. ii. 11).

# CHAPTER IV.

*THAT A PASTOR SHOULD STUDY TO ACQUIRE SUCH
KNOWLEDGE AS SHALL BE PROFITABLE BOTH
TO HIMSELF AND TO HIS HEARERS.*

1. WE cannot all of us do all things (St. Jerome,
Ep. 34 ad Nepot. No. 9). One is, as it
were, an eye in the Church, another a
tongue, others a hand, or a foot, or an ear, or the
interior parts, and so on. See in the Epistle of Paul
to the Corinthians how divers members constitute but
one body (1 Cor. xii. 12 et seqq.). But let not the
ignorant and unlettered brother fancy himself the holier,
simply because he is ignorant; nor let him that is
eloquent and ready of tongue regard *that* qualification
as sanctity. It is much the better of the two imperfect
conditions that a man should be possessed of a holy
rusticity of style than of a sinful eloquence. Reading
is doubtless useful (St. Jerome, ad Nepot. No. 9), and
so is learning, but much more essential is holy unction,
which by itself "teacheth us all things" (St. Chrys. ii. 27);
"but if the blind lead the blind, shall they not both fall
into the ditch" (Matt. xv. 14)?

2. I am well aware (St. Bern. Serm. 36 in Cant. No. 2)
of the advantages conferred upon the Church by learned

Priests, whether in their refutation of adversaries or in
their instruction of the ignorant. I read, "Because
thou hast rejected knowledge, I will also reject thee,
that thou shalt not serve before Me" (Hosea iv. 6).
And I read again, "They that be wise shall shine as
the brightness of the firmament, and they that turn
many to righteousness as the stars for ever and ever"
(Dan. xii. 3). But I know also where I read again that
"knowledge puffeth up" (1 Cor. viii. 1), and again that,
"In much wisdom is much grief, and he that increaseth
knowledge increaseth sorrow" (Eccles. i. 18). You see
there are two kinds of knowledge—one that puffeth up,
and another that causeth sadness. Tell me which of
these you think the preferable or more necessary to
salvation, that which puffs up or that which saddens?
I doubt not you will choose the latter. For that sound
condition of soul which pride can only simulate, sadness
of heart on the contrary rather seeks to possess. And
it is written, "He that seeketh, findeth" (Matt. vii. 8).

Be studious, then, to be acquainted first of all, and
the more thoroughly of all, with what is most helpful
to the salvation of souls. "He that thinketh he knoweth
anything, knoweth nothing yet as he ought to know"
(1 Cor. viii. 2). There are those who desire to know
with the sole object of knowing. This is a miserable
curiosity. Others like to know that they may be known
themselves. This is a sordid vanity. Others, again,
seek knowledge as a profitable concern, in one way or
another. This, too, is a base mode of gain. But there
are those who desire to know that they may edify others

by their knowledge; and this is charity (1 Cor. viii. 1). But there is another case still—that of those who desire to know, that they may be edified themselves ; and this is prudence.   Of all these motives the two last named are alone free from the charge of being an abuse of knowledge, seeing that the end in both cases is beneficent.

## CHAPTER V.

----

*THE STUDY OF HOLY SCRIPTURE, RECOMMENDED TO ALL PASTORS.*

----

1. ALL will be done well by the Priest (St. Greg. Mag. de cur. past. ii. ch. 41) if, influenced solely by the fear and love of God, *he will meditate daily and devoutly on the precepts of Holy Scripture.* And his purpose in doing this will be that the words of Divine warning and instruction therein contained may renew in him the energy of religious earnestness, and the circumspection necessary for the advancement of the heavenly life, which is so constantly being weakened by contact with the world ; so that, whereas on the one side he is constantly being drawn towards the life of the old man by the society of the worldly, he may be restored to the fuller love of the celestial country by the profitable exercise of compunction. For the heart becomes seriously weakened by contact with the world, and while it is past all question that, under these worldly influences, it falls away rapidly from itself, it becomes the more necessary that he should lift it up again by renewed study. Hence Paul saith to his disciple who was set over his flock, " Till I come again give thy diligence to reading " (1 Tim. iv. 13).

2. The careful study of the Divine Scriptures is of immense benefit (St. Chyrs. hom. 35 in Gen. No. 1). It serves to invest the soul with the best moral principles ; it lifts the mind heavenwards, and keeps a man in remembrance of his spiritual blessings. It prevents our being over-fond of temporal things, and fixes our thoughts on the life to come and on the rewards promised to us by Almighty God, which we are thus incited to labour for, and to undertake with a ready mind the arduous pursuit of virtue. From the Scriptures we may readily learn much about the over-ruling providence of God, about the fortitude of the righteous, and about the goodness of God to them, and the greatness of His rewards in store for them. Hence we are the more readily stirred up to follow the example of saintly men, and not to diminish our efforts after a holy life, but to expect with a good and lively hope the reward promised by God.

There is no manner of doubt (St. Aug. Ep. 21 ad Valer. No. 4) that in the Holy Scriptures are to be found the counsels with which, when once duly learned and understood, the " man of God " may be enabled to minister in all ordinary ecclesiastical matters, or, at the least, either to live with a better conscience in the midst of the wicked, or so to die that his life may not be lost, but that humble and Christian hearts may aspire to imitate it.

3. Give heed to the virtue of Holy Scripture and to the efficacy of the Word of God (Pet. Blois, Ep. 140 ad Pet. cler. Angl.), to the due understanding of which

I counsel thee to gird thyself up in fear and trembling.
The Truth saith in the Gospel, " Blessed are they which
hear the word of God and keep it " (Luke xi. 28).   The
chief of the Apostles also, on the Lord's interrogating
His disciples as to whether they would forsake Him,
said, " Lord, to whom shall we go ?   Thou hast the
words of eternal life " (John vi. 69).   Note, too, that
the words of the confession by which the same Apostle
acknowledged Him to be the Son of God, were not
revealed to him by flesh and blood, but by the Spirit
of the Father (Matt. xvi. 17).   And lastly, the words
of God are so spiritual and life-giving, that they are
called both " Spirit and Life ; " as the Lord bare witness, when He said, " The words which I speak unto
you they are Spirit, and they are Life " (John vi. 64).
As the Apostle also saith, " The Word of God is quick
and powerful, and like a two-edged sword, reaching to
the very dividing asunder of the soul and spirit, and of
the joints and marrow " (Hebr. iv. 12).   And why is
this, but that it possesses the nature of some powerful
potion, by which all noxious conditions are eliminated
from the human spirit, and wholly purged away.

And that experience may the more convince you of
this truth, if you are doubtful of it, set yourself to read
the Holy Scriptures still more diligently, and learn that
the Word of God can set your soul on fire.   If you are
walking in darkness, hear what the Lord saith to thee
in the Gospel and in the Prophets, and His Word will
be " a lantern unto thy feet and a light unto thy paths "
(Ps. cxix. 105).   If you have contracted any stain of sin,

the Word of Christ will cleanse you ; as He saith, "Ye are clean, because of the Word which I have spoken unto you" (John xv. 3). If some severe temptation assail you, so that you seem almost to be losing your footing (Ps. lxxiii. 2), the Word of God will strengthen and support you, that you may not fall. For what can be more powerful than that of which we read that "By the Word of the Lord were the *heavens made*, and all the host of them by the Breath of His mouth" (Ps. xxxiii. 6)? If you be in mortal sin, which is the death of the soul, Holy Scripture will revive thee, and that will be fulfilled which the Lord saith in the Gospel :—"The hour cometh, and now is, when the dead shall hear the Voice of the Son of God, and they that hear shall live" (John v. 25). And this you may be well assured of, that the Holy Spirit uttered and set forth *both* Testaments, and fitted them the one to the other with the skill of an inconceivable wisdom ;—as there appeared (we read) to the Prophet Ezekiel "wheels within wheels ; and they were both lifted up together, and they went together, and the spirit of life was in the wheels" (Ezek. i. 19 and 20 ; cf. Greg. Mag. in locum).

4. Some one may possibly ask (St. Aug. de doctr. Christ. lib. iv. 6. 9) whether the inspired writers of Holy Scripture are to be considered as wise only, or also as eloquent. It is my own opinion, and that of my companions with me, that the question may be readily answered. For when I once come to understand their writings, it appears to me, not only that nothing exists which is more full of wisdom, but also

nothing that is more truly eloquent. And I venture to say that all persons who correctly understand what they have said, will perceive also that they ought not to have said anything else. There is a certain eloquent style which more properly becomes young persons, and another which becomes aged persons, and *that* cannot be called eloquence which does not accord with the age of the speaker. So, again, there is an eloquence which suits men worthy of high places of authority, and especially divines. And just so do these holy writers speak. Anything else would not have suited them ; and what they have said would have suited no one else ; for it suits *them* exactly. But in proportion as it may appear to some to be too inferior a style, so much the higher does it stand, not indeed in inflation, but in *solidity*. But where I cannot understand them, their eloquence seems to me to be inferior ; yet I doubt not that it is the same, too, as it is when I do understand them. Their very obscurity, it would seem, had to be expressed in such a style of eloquence as should advance our intelligence, not only in the way of research, but of practical application.

# CHAPTER VI.

*FURTHER REMARKS ON THE STUDY OF HOLY SCRIPTURE.*

1. BE often occupied in the study of the Holy Scriptures (St. Jerome, Ep. 34 ad Nepot. No. 7). Nay, let them never leave thy hands.* Learn there what thou art to teach. Hold fast that which is according to sound doctrine and faithful discourse, that you may teach others the same, and convince the gainsayers (Tit. i. 9). " Continue in that which thou hast learned, and which is committed unto thee, knowing from whom thou hast learned it (2 Tim. iii. 14), and be always ready to give an answer to him that asketh thee a reason of the hope that is in thee with meekness and fear " (1 Pet. iii. 15).

Become acquainted with the Mind and Will of God in His Word (St. Greg. Mag. Ep. xxxi. 4. 12) that you may aspire the more ardently after eternal things, and that your mind may be inflamed with more earnest desires after the joys of Heaven.

We should brood over, and *wear out*, as it were, the

---

* Such is said to have been practically the case with the late Rev. Dr. Cotton, Provost of Worcester College, Oxford. It was doubtless rarely off his table, if ever.

Divine sayings of Scripture; letting our whole hearts and minds become familiar with them, that the spiritual juice of that heavenly food may penetrate our whole soul.

2. So great is the depth of the Christian Scriptures (St. Aug. Ep. 37 ad Volusianum), that I should every day have been adding more and more to my knowledge of them, even were I to have studied them and nothing else every day of my life from my childhood to a ripe old age; and *that* with the full command of my time, with the most careful study, and with the highest natural abilities. I do not mean to say that, to arrive at a knowledge of the Holy Scriptures sufficient for our salvation, so much study is necessary; but that, when a man has once placed his devout confidence in them, without which he cannot live uprightly and religiously, there is so much depth of meaning ever to be discerned and understood in them, as he advances in his study of them—and *that* not merely of their language, but of their still more obscure matter—that what the Scripture itself says is true of the most long-lived, the most acute, and the most earnest pursuers of knowledge, viz., that "When a man has ended, then he begins" (Ecclus. xviii. 6).

3. Holy Scripture is a Divine sea (St. Ambr. Ep. 2 ad Const. Episc. 3 and 4), having in itself deep meanings, and most subtle prophetic enigmas—a sea whereinto there flows many a river (Eccles. i. 7). Consequently there are therein many pure and delicious streams, and many snow-white and gushing fountains, which spring forth into eternal life (John iv. 14).

There are glowing discourses savouring of honey, and grateful sentiments which refresh the reader's minds as with a kind of spiritual draught, and soothe them with the refreshing sweetness of their moral precepts. Diverse, therefore, are the streams which flow from the Holy Scriptures. Treasure up, then, I pray you, what you first drink—treasure up what you drink further on, and treasure up your very latest found draughts of sacred knowledge.

Gather up the water of Christ (John vii. 38), which is the glory of God (Ps. cxlviii. 4). Gather water from every source, such as the laden clouds of prophecy pour forth. He that draws water from the mountains, and applies it to his own use, or, draws it straight from the running streams, he shall himself also drop dew like the clouds. Fill the lap, then, of your mind, that your soil may become moist, and be watered from your own wells. He that reads much, and understands what he reads, shall himself be filled (Matt. xxiv. 15); and he that has been so filled, will *water others*. Hence the Scripture itself saith : " If the clouds be full of rain, they will empty themselves upon the earth " (Eccles. xi. 3).

4. A man will speak and teach well (St. Aug. de doct. Christ. iv. 5) in proportion as he is a proficient in the study of the Holy Scriptures. I do not mean in merely reading them frequently, or in committing them to memory, but in thoroughly understanding them, and in searching diligently into their inner meaning. For there are some who read the Scriptures, but neglect them when read. They read them that they may

L

retain them in their memory; but they neglect their deeper study, so as not fully to understand them. Far preferable to such as these are those who read them less, but see with their aid into the secrets of their own hearts. But he is better than both these, who can cite them when he will, and understand them as he ought. The man, therefore, whose office it is to teach them wisely, albeit he cannot do so eloquently, is more especially bound to keep the *words* of Scripture in his memory. For in proportion as he perceives his own words to be poor and feeble, the more should he enrich himself with the words of Scripture; so that what he says in his own words he may prove by the words of Scripture, and what may seem feeble when expressed in his own language, may grow in his hearers' estimation by the testimony of those greater words.[*]

At the reading of the Gospel in the Divine Office (Hildebrand, Serm. xciii. 6), the Book of the Gospels is given open to the Priests to be kissed, but to others it is given closed. As though at that very time it was being said to him, "It is given to thee to know the mysteries of the kingdom of God, but to others in parables" (Luke viii. 10).

---

[*] The Translator would desire at this point to call attention to the order of our Prayer-book, that "all Priests and Deacons are to say daily the Morning and Evening Prayer, either privately or openly, not being let by sickness or some other urgent cause."

And the Curate that ministereth in every Parish Church or Chapel, being at home, and not being otherwise reasonably hindered, shall say the same in the Parish Church or Chapel where he ministereth, and shall cause a bell to be tolled thereunto a convenient time before he begins, that the people may come to hear God's Word, and to pray with him.

But I fear (Origen, hom. xii. in Exod. xxxiv. De velo Moysis) lest, by over much negligence and dulness of heart, the Divine Scriptures are not only apt to be concealed from us, but even to be sealed against us. It follows, therefore, that not only should much diligence be applied to the study of Holy Scripture, but that prayer should be offered up to God, night and day, that the " Lamb of the tribe of Judah " should Himself take up the sealed Book, and graciously open it for us (Rev. v. 5). For He it is, Who, by opening for us the Divine Scriptures, will kindle the hearts of His disciples, so that they shall say, " Did not our hearts burn within us, as He opened unto us the Scriptures" (Luke xxiv. 32)?

5. Do not be satisfied merely to turn over the leaves of the Book, but rather, if need be, do not be unwilling to repeat a passage two or three times over, or even oftener, that you may arrive at its true significance.

When, therefore, you are preparing to read the Holy Scriptures or to hear them read to you, offer up a prayer to God and say, " O Lord Jesus Christ, open the ears and the eyes of my heart, that I may hear and understand Thy Word, and obey Thy Will. For I am an inhabitant of the earth ; hide not therefore from me Thy commandments. Open Thou mine eyes that I may understand the wondrous things of Thy Law " (Ps. cxix. 18).

6. In your interpretation of Holy Scripture nothing need be rejected which is not actually opposed to sound faith. For as from one mass of gold some will make ear-rings, others finger-rings, and others bracelets, and

all for the purpose of ornament; so, out of passages of Holy Scripture, some will draw one conclusion and some another, and men of different turns of mind will interpret and illustrate them in different ways, yet all alike *to the glory of the celestial Spouse.*[*]

## CONCLUSION.

To conclude, then, my brethren, meditate, I beseech you, on these weighty matters. Consider them carefully with yourselves, and enjoin the practices here recommended to you upon your friends and acquaintances. Prepare to give an account to Almighty God of the task which you have undertaken, but remember that you will obtain the graces of which we have here spoken, by *praying* rather than by *talking*.

## PRAYER.

O God, Who hast willed to call us Thy servants to be Pastors among Thy people, grant, we beseech Thee, that what we are so called by the lips of men, we may have grace to prove ourselves to be in Thine own sight, through Jesus Christ our Lord. Amen.

### LAUS DEO.

---

[*] The Translator has purposely forborne from *any* abridgement of these latter passages, with the view of disarming any persons who may fancy, as some seem to do, that the study of the FATHERS is injurious to that of the HOLY SCRIPTURES.

# APPENDIX:

1. TERTULLIAN, a Priest of Carthage, died A.D. 245. St. Cyprian used to call Tertullian his father. His chief works are the "Apology;" "On repentance;" "On public shows;" "On the veiling of Virgins;" "A treatise against Marcion;" "On the Flesh of Christ;" "On the Resurrection of Christ;" "On Prescriptions;" "On the Testimony of the Soul;" "On Prayer," and "On Patience." The character of his works changed on his secession to Montanism, after which they must be read with caution.

2. ORIGEN, Priest of Alexandria, died A.D. 253. The best work of Origen is generally considered to be that "Against Celsus." To this may be added his "Exhortation to Martyrdom," his Treatise "On Prayer," his "Refutation of Heresies," and his "Commentaries on Holy Scripture" (of which only a portion remains), and particularly that on the Song of Solomon. His knowledge of Holy Scripture was truly remarkable.

3. ST. CYPRIAN, Bishop of Carthage, Martyr A.D. 258. The principal works of this Father are "On the Unity of the Church," "On the Lord's Prayer," "On almsgiving," "On the Dress of Virgins," "On Envy," "On the fallen," and "On Mortality." The work attributed to him, and entitled "De Singularitate Clericorum," is apocryphal.

4. St. Athanasius, Patriarch of Alexandria, died A.D. 378. The works of this Father are almost entirely devoted to the Arian controversy, in which he was the foremost defender of the Catholic Faith. His style is good, and his arguments cogent and convincing. His five orations against the Arians are of the highest excellence, both for eloquence and for learning. Next to these, his Commentary on the Psalms stands pre-eminent, and deserves careful study.

5. St. Ephraim, Deacon of Edessa, died A.D. 379. St. Jerome calls this Father a divine scribe (De viris illustribus c. 115). His principal works are his Sermons on Piety, his commentaries on the historical Books of Holy Scripture and on the Prophets, and his controversial works against the heretics. His "Discourse on the Priesthood" was formerly made an appendix, or seventh book, to that of St. Chrysostom on the same subject.

6. St. Basil the Great, Bishop of Cæsarea, died A.D. 379. The letters of this Doctor are recommended by Photius as models of the epistolary style ; Erasmus and Rollin place him in the first rank of orators. Nothing, says Fenelon, could be more eloquent than his letter to a Virgin who had fallen. His style is pure, precise, clear and without fault. His Hexameron, his Homilies, in which he adheres strictly to the literal sense of the Scriptures, and his moral treatises on gluttony and drunkenness, as well as his Panegyrics, should especially be read.

7. St. Gregory Nazianzen, Abp. of Constantinople, died A.D. 389. The soundness of this Father's doctrine and the loftiness of his thoughts have earned for him the name of "Theologian." The brightness and ease, and the grace and eloquence of his style are conspicuous in all his writings. The

richness of his imagination, possibly somewhat excessive, has
led him to indulge in a profusion of ornaments and figures.
His discourses on the Priesthood, delivered at Constantinople,
his Eulogies of St. Cæsarius and St. Athanasius, the greater
part of his letters, and the poem which he wrote on his own life,
are especially worthy of study.

8. St. GREGORY, Bishop of Nyssa, died A.D. 396. Brother
to St. Basil the Great, Gregory of Nyssa became nearly his
equal, both in reputation and in the authority of his writings;
but he did not equal him in his exquisite style. His principal
works are his controversies with Eumenius, his Hexameron,
his treatises on the Creation of man, on Prayer, and on the
Beatitudes.

9. St. AMBROSE, Bishop of Milan, died A.D. 397. In the
works of St. Ambrose generally there are everywhere to be
found the marks of a noble spirit, lofty in thought, full of zeal
for the Church, love for the poor, and compassion towards
sinners. His style is weighty, nervous, concise and sententious.
Nowhere do we meet with maxims more cogent and to the
point; but his brevity at times is a cause of some obscurity
and difficulty. He was deeply learned in Holy Scripture, and
especially in the Old Testament, on which he spent much
labour. His works De Officiis, the Hexameron, the lives of
the Patriarchs, and that on Virginity are the most prominent,
together with the Commentary on St. Luke. The treatise on
"The dignity of the Priestly Office," cited as his in this book,
is aprocryphal, and probably of a late date, as is also the letter
ascribed to him, "Ad Virginem devotam."

10. St. JOHN CHRYSOSTOM, Archbishop of Constantinople,
died A.D. 407. Bossuet has described this Father as "the

Christian Demosthenes," and as being, past all contradiction, the most distinguished writer in the Church ; as a man, too, of happy genius, born, as it were, to strike home and to convince,— a judicious and wise spirit, endowed with a brilliant and fertile imagination, ever noble and ever bright, profuse without per- plexity, and the best model that can be set before Christian orators. His quotations of Scripture are singularly apt, as was his power of eliciting deep meanings from them. Among his best works are his treatise " De Sacerdotio," his Homilies on the Epistles of St. Paul, especially those to the Romans and Corinthians, his commentaries on St. Matthew, on Genesis and Isaiah, and his treatise on " The Statues." That on St. Matthew, however, entitled " Opus imperfectum," is of doubtful genuineness.

11. ST. JEROME, Priest, died A.D. 420. The labours of St. Jerome were chiefly devoted to the text of the Holy Scriptures; but he has also left behind him other works both of merit and importance. "His style," says Fenelon, "is masculine and lofty, and more eloquent than that of many who would have their own to be so regarded." His powerful imagination and natural sternness give to his eloquence a sort of roughness which takes one by surprise, and a vigour which seems to knock one down. His principal works are his " Letters " and his " Com- mentaries on Holy Scripture," especially those on the Prophets.

12. ST. AUGUSTINE, Bishop of Hippo, died A.D. 430. This Father is especially noted for the universality of his talents, his acute penetration, his fertile industry, his sensitive disposition, his modesty, piety, humility, and sweetness of temper. Of his works, Bossuet especially recommends for study his " De Doc- trinâ Christianâ," his treatise " De catechizandis rudibus," his " Manuale ad Laurentium," " On the Spirit and the Letter,"

"On true religion," and "On the City of God." To these may be added his "Confessions," his Sermons and his Treatise on morality. "His style," says Fenelon, "is at once sublime and popular. He ascends by the most ordinary stages to the noblest heights. He puts questions only to answer them, and seems to be holding conversations with his readers; but one's attention is wholly carried away from the consideration of his style by the depth and greatness of his conclusions."

13. St. Paulinus, Bishop of Nola, died A.D. 431. The remains of this Holy Bishop consist chiefly of poetical pieces, letters and discourses, of a dignified, but ornamental and pleasing character. Especially prominent are his discourse on Almsgiving, and several of his Letters; of which St. Augustine says that they possess the sweetness of milk and honey.

14. St. Cyril of Alexandria, died A.D. 444. This Father is not signalized by excellence of method, nor by elegance of style, nor even by his choice of thoughts; but he is to be recommended for the exactness of his teaching, the correctness of his reasoning, and by an uncommon degree of learning. The works of his most to be recommended are his "Thesaurus" and his "Letters" against Nestorius and against Julian the Apostate.

15. St. Eucherius, Bishop of Lyons, died A.D. 454. One of the purest and most elegant of the Latin Fathers. His chief works are "On the contempt of the world," "On the solitary life," and his "Institutions," in which he solves some difficulties presented by the reading of Holy Scripture.

16. St. Prosper of Aquitania, died A.D. 463. The writings left us by this Father consist of a poem against the "Ungrateful," by whom he means the Pelagians, who denied the need of the

M

gift of grace ; also sundry pieces of poetry, and some prose works of value. But the work cited as his, and entitled, " On the contemplative and active life," was written by a contemporary of his, Julian Pomerius.

17. St. Gregory the Great, Pope, died A.D. 604. The special merit and characteristics of this Father, are, his perfect knowledge of the human heart and of Christian morals, a tender piety united with an exquisite judgment, a discreet zeal and a boundless charity, great boldness and a charming modesty. His style, almost always simple, is sometimes careless. " Born in a barbarous age," observes Fenelon, " this Father has nevertheless written much that is of a superior character and style." His " De curâ Pastorali " should by all means be read,* and is described by Bossuet as a work of the very highest merit. It is recommended by several of the councils, and especially so to Bishops on their consecration. His other works are " Letters to Ecclesiastics," " Homilies on the Gospels," and the " Morals of the Book of Job."

18. St. Isidore, Bishop of Seville, died A.D. 656. St. Isidore of Seville was the most learned man of his time, and was for thirty years regarded as the oracle of Spain. His writings contain many valuable directions and pious instructions. His style is clear and simple, but somewhat irregular and diffuse. His book on the duties of Ecclesiastics should be read, in which he describes the several parts of the Divine Office.

19. St. Bernard of Clairvaux, died A.D. 1153. St. Bernard (writes Fenelon) was a prodigy in a barbarous age.

---

* This work has been ably translated by the Rev. Preb. Bramley, of Magdalen College, Oxford (Parkers), the Latin also being given on the opposite page.

His learning, his piety, his ardent zeal, his exquisite taste, and the natural grace and simplicity of His style, raise him to such a high rank among the Doctors of the Church, as to place him above those even of the best periods of the Church's History. He has none of the dryness of his predecessors. The vivacity, the sweetness, the unction and the energy, which characterize all his discourses are conspicuous. His humility and charity are constantly observable in the touching sentences which proceed from his pen, while at the same time his perfect command of the Holy Scriptures seems to supply him at any moment with the most apt allusions and allegories. No writer has ever expressed the emotions of the heart, or those of true spiritual unction and piety better than he. He constrains us to love him, even while aiming at us the most powerful blows, and we discover, as we read him, the source of the extraordinary influence which he exercised in his day over every rank in the Church.

Ecclesiastics should carefully study his works, but especially his treatise "On Consideration," frequently quoted in this work—his "Manners and duties of a Bishop," addressed to Henry, Archbishop of Sens—his "treatise on the conversion of clerks"—his "Letters," and his "Sermons on the Song of Solomon," and on the "Mysteries."

The treatise "On the Contempt of the world," which has been placed among his apocryphal works, is the work of Ganfride, his pupil and secretary. Mabillon entitles it, "Declamations on the conversation between Simon Peter and Jesus." The two discourses, "On the Council of Rheims," and "In Synod," are likewise Apocryphal.

20. PETER DE BLOIS, Archdeacon of Bath, and afterwards of London, died circ. A.D. 1200. This devout Doctor mani-

fested as much zeal for discipline as he did little for ecclesiastical promotion. In his youth (he says) he found a great charm in the writings of Hildebert, and from this circumstance he seems to have imbibed both his spirit and his zeal. He read with the like perseverance and study the works of the principal Fathers, and he has left us the fruit of these readings and meditations in a large number of letters and several sermons. Although he had less unction than power, and his style is somewhat overstrained, his letters do not fail to afford to Ecclesiastics a valuable treasury of instruction and good advice.

"Tunc Sacerdos irreprehensibiliter graditur cum exemplo Patrum precedentium indesinenter intuetur, et sanctorum vestigia sine cessatione considerat" (St. Greg. Mag. Ep. xxv. ad Johannem, Episcopum Constantinopolitanum).

The Editor is not to be considered responsible for the correctness of the particulars above recorded, of which he has only undertaken the responsibility of a Translator.